# STRENGTH: MY MEMOIR

By Mira Rosenblatt

with Belinda Rosenblatt Levavi

MEMOIRS PLUS

www.memoirsplus.com

ISBN: 9798697702673

# TABLE OF CONTENTS

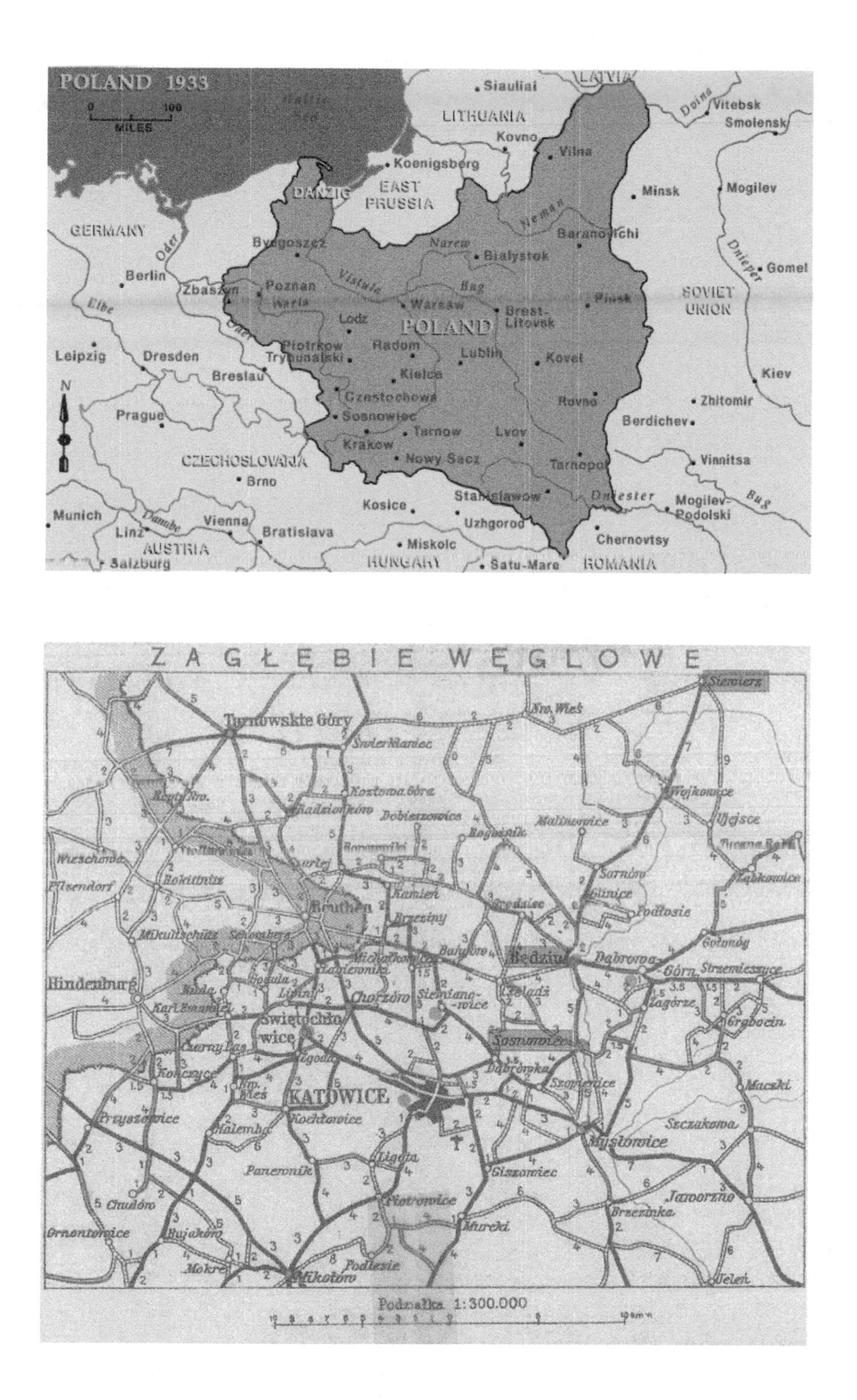
POLAND 1933
MILES
LATVIA
Siauliai
LITHUANIA
Kovno
Vilna
Vitebsk
Smolensk
Koenigsberg
DANZIG
EAST PRUSSIA
Minsk
Mogilev
GERMANY
Oder
Bydgoszcz
Narew
Bialystok
Neman
Berlin
Zbaszyn
Poznan
Warta
Vistula
Bug
Warsaw
Brest-Litovsk
Pinsk
SOVIET UNION
Gomel
Dnieper
Elbe
Lodz
POLAND
Piotrkow Trybunalski
Radom
Lublin
Kovel
Leipzig
Dresden
Breslau
Kielce
Kiev
Czestochowa
Rovno
Zhitomir
Prague
Sosnowiec
Tarnow
Lvov
Berdichev
Krakow
Nowy Sacz
Tarnopol
Vinnitsa
CZECHOSLOVAKIA
Brno
Stanislawow
Dniester
Mogilev-Podolski
Kosice
Munich
Danube
Vienna
Linz
Bratislava
Uzhgorod
Chernovtsy
AUSTRIA
Miskolc
Salzburg
HUNGARY
Satu-Mare
ROMANIA
N
ZAGŁĘBIE WĘGLOWE
Siewierz
Tarnowskie Góry
Świerklaniec
Kozłowa Góra
Radzionków
Dobieszowice
Malinowice
Wojkowice
Ujejsce
Rogoźnik
Sarnów
Bokittnitz
Kamień
Brzeziny
Grodziec
Podłosie
Beuthen
Mikultschütz
Będzin
Dąbrowa
Golonóg
Hindenburg
Czeladź
Chorzów
Lipiny
Świętochłowice
Sosnowiec
Strzemieszyce
Zagórze
Grabocin
Czarny Las
Dąbrówka
Szopienice
KATOWICE
Kochłowice
Halemba
Przyszowice
Mysłowice
Maczki
Szczakowa
Ligota
Panewnik
Giszowiec
Piotrowice
Jaworzno
Brzezinka
Murcki
Chudów
Ornontowice
Bujaków
Mokre
Mikołów
Podlesie
Jeleń
Podziałka 1:300.000

## PREFACE

# ALWAYS LOOKING TOWARD TOMORROW

I have never hesitated to tell my stories of the Holocaust. It has been my personal mission since I survived such horrendous atrocities to let people hear directly from me what I witnessed during World War II. I have literally told thousands of people my stories and know that, despite the difficult emotions it stirs in me, I am fortunate to remember in detail, even as I reach my late nineties, how much I saw, felt, and experienced as a young girl. As survivors of the Holocaust are becoming fewer and fewer, I want my future generations to know what our families had to endure and to remember all that has been lost.

My children and grandchildren have heard my stories—it has been my calling. Even at young ages, I told them of the horrors of living in Poland and working in a labor camp as part of a concentration camp. Some survivors never wished to speak about it, but I found it helpful for me to let others know what I saw and how I had the individual strength to carry on when I lost so many close family members, including my parents and most of my siblings and extended family. I am fortunate to have preserved these memories, as they are all I have left of my family. I brought my children back to Poland and Germany to see firsthand where my husband, a fellow survivor, and I had lived and where we had suffered.

I have often wondered how I survived while so many didn't and I have struggled with a way to understand the reason. I have no way to answer that question. When the war ended, I weighed sixty-eight pounds and had all of my hair cut off. I had trouble walking and have been in physical pain since then. Sometimes I wondered how I was able to become part of the living and was able to embrace life after all that I had gone through—I know it was because of my husband, Henry Rosenblatt, an Auschwitz survivor. He found me after the war and never stopped loving me and taking care of me. He gave me the strength to continue living and loving. We were together for seventy-one years, from 1945 until his death in 2017.

G-d punished me with different things but he also blessed me with many things and helped me survive, for a reason, to tell my story with my vivid memories. These memories helped me gain the strength to survive. I truly believe I have been saved to tell my story.

# PART I:

# STAY STRONG AND HOPE

# CHAPTER 1

# SOSNOWIEC

## My Neighborhood

My name is Mira Rosenblatt and I am a survivor of the Holocaust and life. I was born in Sosnowiec, Poland, on November 29, 1923, but on all of my official papers, I was born on May 20, 1923. I have strong and clear memories of my wonderful childhood from six years old on. And I have strong and clear memories of the horrors I went through during the Holocaust. G-d had granted me long years and I have lived my life to the fullest, but it is time for me to write my story for my grandchildren, great-grandchildren, and future generations to know and to remember. Please never forget.

I lived in the southwest part of Poland in the province known as the Zaglembie region. My city, Sosnowiec, was close to the German border and, because of this, we dealt with Germans all the time. We walked back and forth to Germany and Germans came back and forth to Sosnowiec. Sosnowiec was in an industrial area and had textile and leather factories, but more importantly, it had coal mines, quarries, and farms. When World War II broke out, Germany immediately annexed the Zaglembie region because of its valuable economic resources. The Jews and all their possessions then became the property of the Third Reich and the Jews were used as slave laborers.

Sosnowiec [1] had about 180,000 people living there and about 20 percent of the people were Jews. It was between Katowice and Będzin. All three cities had large Jewish populations who were mostly Yiddish-speaking religious Jews. Sosnowiec had important rebbes like the Radomska Rebbe, the Alexander Rebbe, and the Kozhnitzer Rebbe, and many yeshivas. However, there were all kinds of Jews besides Chassidim living in my city: Orthodox, Reform, Zionists, Bundists, Socialists, and Communists. There was a lot of interaction among the Jewish communities of Sosnowiec, Będzin, and Katowice because we were so close to each other.

I had a wonderful childhood. I had a lot of freedom and went everywhere around the city. I visited my aunts and uncles and other relatives who all lived around the area. We walked everywhere because nobody had cars so either you walked or, if you were older, you took the trolley. I spoke Polish and Yiddish and a decent German.

My first home was in Stary Sosnowiec on Piłsudska 64 Street on the corner of Składowa Street in a thirty-nine-tenant apartment building my grandfather built. Piłsudska was a main street in the older part of the city named for the Polish prime minister, Josef Piłsudska. This is where I grew up and had all my happy childhood memories.

In the streets around Piłsudska and Składowa, there was a walled-off

---

[1] Sosnowiec was located in Upper Silesia right on the border of Germany and was occupied in the first days of the war. It was a heavily industrialized area with many coal mines. It was situated in the Incorporated Territories of the Third Reich, known as the Zaglembie region. Unlike in other Polish areas, the Nazis themselves governed Zaglembie and the swastika adorned much of the area's documentation. Zaglembie was seen as vital to the German war machine, and there were conflicting views within the Nazi regime as to how the Jews living in this area should be dealt with. The extermination of the Jews remained the primary Nazi objective. However, the Schmelt Organization, a Nazi agency that supervised the use of slave labor, utilized many of the Silesian Jews. Therefore, many Jews in this region took winding routes to Auschwitz; many were held captive in slave labor satellite camps connected to Auschwitz before the final deportation. Zev Levavi, "Chil Rosenblatt: A Survivor's Story" (unpublished).

convent for nuns, two synagogues, and the new Jewish business school near Wiejska Street. This trade school opened right before the war and later was used by the Nazis as a transit center—to assemble the Jews for deportation. It became known as the infamous "Dulag."

Our apartment was on the first floor and had two large rooms with big windows: a dining room and a bedroom, and then the kitchen where we spent most of our time. The kitchen was also used as a bedroom with two big beds in the corner; I slept in one bed with my sisters Vida Malka and Estusha; and my baby brother, Natan, and our maid, Marisha, slept in the other bed. The bedroom was divided by curtains and my parents slept in one corner and my two older brothers, Herschel and Manek, slept in the other corner. The dining room had a large dining room table where we ate on Shabbos. On the half floors there were bathrooms to wash up in and we used an outhouse in the courtyard.

On the street of Składowa was a big garden, which was the backyard to my apartment building. You needed special permission to go into the garden, but because I lived in the building, I could go in whenever I wanted to. The garden was very beautiful with fruit trees and vegetables and flowers. I loved the smell and taste of the strawberries and my older sister loved the sunflowers. In one part of the garden, there was an area where they fixed wagons and shoed horses.

I was a ringleader in the neighborhood and a real tomboy. The neighborhood kids, both Jewish and Polish, knocked on my window and called out: "Mira, come out! Come out! Play with us!" I played jump rope, hide-and-seek, and other games. Sometimes the Polish boys got wild and were mean to the Jewish kids. I punished them by locking them in the shed when they got like that.

Across the street there was a large field that was used for baseball and other sports. A few streets away was a real sports stadium where they had sports matches. Sometimes, I would sneak over the fence with my friends to watch the games.

My childhood neighborhood played a very important part in my story and that is why I am describing it in such detail. The stadium, the garden, the business school, my neighbors—all played critical roles later on. My wonderful memories were destroyed by the events that took place right where I grew up and showed how the Holocaust was deeply personal to each and every one of us. It did not take place among strangers or in strange places; it happened right in our homes with people and places we were most familiar with.

## My Parents and Grandparents

My father was Shlomo Itzhak Rosenblatt and his family were Alexander Chassidim from Będzin. His father was Nutur Rosenblatt. I didn't know my father's parents so well because they lived in a different town and died young. My father was very distinguished looking; he was tall and had a gray beard and wore a hat with a small brim. He put on tefillin every morning and davened/prayed and was always learning Torah when he wasn't working. He was chassidish and religious but at the same time was part of the modern world.

My mother was Helena (Hendel) Lenczycki and she was from Sosnowiec. She was very beautiful and was considered a kokietka, a modern, elegant, sophisticated woman. She dressed stylishly and covered her hair with a wig/sheitel. She never went outside in a teichel (kerchief). My mother was the only one of her sisters who wore a sheitel; they were more modern in their religious practices.

My mother's parents were Mordechai Wolf Lenczycki and Baila Yehudis Abramowicz. My grandfather, my zaide, came from Lodz and my grandmother, my bubbe, came from Sielec on the outskirts of Sosnowiec. My father married my mother when she was eighteen years old and they moved into their own apartment in the same building as her parents and siblings. We were very close to my grandparents and my uncles and aunts because we all lived together.

My mother, Helena, was the eldest of nine siblings. Her family was religious, and her brothers went to yeshiva. She and her siblings all had a secular education and were well read. My mother was fluent in many languages—Polish, Yiddish, German, and Russian. My mother knew Hebrew so she could daven. She even spoke Esperanto, the language of the Polish clergy, as did all her brothers and sisters. My grandfather had hired special tutors to teach them Esperanto. [2]

My zaide and bubbe were almost like my parents. My zaide was very tall—over six feet—and had a long white beard. He used to put all his grandchildren on his lap and tickle them. My bubbe was short and chubby and hugged us all the time. When I was sick, I stayed in their apartment and they took care of me because my mother was busy with the store and my younger sister and brother. I have a special memory of my grandparents insisting that I stay with them after getting a tooth pulled. They were worried that my parents were too busy to take care of me and give me the right amount of attention.

My grandparents had a factory that made copper pipes that were used for gutters in apartment buildings. They also owned two apartment buildings in Sosnowiec. One was the large thirty-nine-tenant building on Piłsudska Street, which was completed in 1914, right before World War I. During that war, the Germans captured and occupied Sosnowiec. They requisitioned the building and moved their officers into the apartments. Our family was allowed to remain along with some of the other tenants. I wasn't born yet when this happened. [3]

My zaide had a glass eye that he took out every night and put in a glass of water on the windowsill. He lost his eye during World War I when a bomb exploded in our courtyard and hit the giant metal water wheel that pumped water for the building. A piece of metal broke off from the wheel and flew into his eye. Zaide always thought he was lucky that he only lost his eye and wasn't killed. The wheel was connected to a pipe system that let the tenants pump water from an underground well and fill their buckets right there in the courtyard. This was a modern convenience for the times and my zaide was very proud of it.

---

[2] Esperanto was a language meant to foster an international community created by Ludwik Lejzer Zamenhof and was popular in the 1900s.

[3] Poland was part of greater Russia before and during World War I and only gained its independence in 1918. I have a copy of my grandparents' marriage certificate in Russian.

## My Brothers and Sisters

I was the fourth child of six children. I had three brothers and two sisters. First there was my eldest brother Herschel, born in 1917, then Manek, born in 1919, then my older sister Vita Malka born in 1921, then came me, Mira, known as Meera or Mirce, born in 1923, followed by my little sister Esther (Estusha), born in 1930, and my baby brother Natan, born in 1931. I had another brother, Berel, who died as a baby. He was between me and my sister Esther. I don't really remember him, but I remember my mother saying his name.

Herschel and Manek were very close to each other and full of life. They put on tefillin every day and went to yeshiva but also learned secular subjects. They loved to play sports, especially European football. They were boys and older, so they had much more freedom than I did. They went out with friends, both boys and girls, and stayed out late into the night. They knocked on my window and woke me to unlock the main door and let them in. Otherwise, they would have had to wake up the superintendent and pay him for the service. Then my parents would have found out and my brothers would have gotten into trouble. My brothers bribed me to do a lot of things for them, like iron the crease in their pants, take their ripped shoes to the shoemaker—but they never paid up. I didn't really mind because they were so much fun to be around. They were both active in Jewish clubs; Herschel belonged to Mizrachi and Maccabi, which was a Zionist sports club. Manek belonged to Hanoar Hazioni, a Zionist youth group that was less religious.

There was a mandatory draft into the Polish army that was strictly upheld because of the growing fear about war. It was considered the worst thing for a Jewish boy to get drafted because you couldn't remain a Jew. Herschel was called up and we were really scared that he would have to go. My parents did everything possible and somehow kept him out of the army. By this time, my brothers were old enough to work and they both had full-time jobs in textile stores in Sosnowiec; Herschel worked at Olsteins and Manek worked at Ostreichers.

Vida Malka was quiet and ladylike. She was a good student and read books all the time. We were very different. She was sensitive and nervous, not like me who was a tomboy and fearless. I moved like lightning and she moved slowly. Vida Malka stayed separate from the Polish kids because they teased her a lot and even bullied her. She didn't like that they were so wild and rude to each other and she hated that they pulled up all the flowers in the garden. One Passover during the part of the seder when we opened the door for Eliyahu, I walked in wearing a white sheet and Vida Malka got so scared that she fainted. I got into a lot of trouble for this. Vida Malka had a very hard time during the war because she was so nervous and fearful.

Estusha and Natan were sweet, happy little kids. They were one and half years apart and were inseparable. They hung on me and followed me around because they thought I was fun to be with. Estusha was very bright and mature for her age, even in the good years. We adored each other and she was always a big help to me. Natan was my baby. He had black hair and eyes with long lashes. I loved to brush his hair and used to part it on the side. Natan hated when people complimented him on how beautiful he was because he was very shy. He was smart as a whip and knew his Alef Bais, how to say Modeh Ani and daven. He sat right next to me every night when I did my homework, pretending to do homework as well.

## Family Life

The family ate breakfast together before school and we ate our main meal together in the afternoon when we got home from school. In the evening, we had something small like a sandwich and everyone ate at different times. This was the European style of eating. I wasn't a good eater but I loved fresh rye bread.

I have beautiful memories of Shabbos, which was such a special time for my family. To this day, I can see my mother lighting the Shabbos candles and smell her Shabbos food and the home-baked challah. The dining room table was set with nice dishes and we were dressed in our nicest clothes. My mother was an excellent baker and everyone loved to eat her cakes. I wasn't such a sweet eater, so I gave my cake to my brothers and made them happy. On

Shabbos day, we picked up our cholent pot from the neighborhood bakery oven where it had cooked all night with all our neighbors' cholent pots. [4] This way we could have something warm to eat since we weren't allowed to cook on Shabbos.

For Passover, the men went to a special bakery and made matzah by hand. They brought back the matzahs in a special basket that my parents stored high up in one of the closets until the seder. We kids always tried to sneak one or two matzahs to eat before the holiday.

My father sat at the head of the dining room table in his special chair and nobody left the table until my father did. No one ever sat in his chair because it would be disrespectful. Everything was about respect. My parents taught us Derech eretz—respect for everyone, especially your parents, grandparents, and older people. My father was strict and we gave him a lot of respect, but he never laid a hand on me and I was a tough kid.

During the week my father davened at home because of the store hours. On Shabbos, he went to Rabbi Englard's shul (synagogue) down the street from us, right next to the new trade school. My brothers and my mother would go to shul but my sister and I and the little ones stayed home and played. I never learned to daven so well because I didn't go to shul regularly. Every week, my parents invited a guest from shul to eat Shabbos lunch with us. There was always someone who had no place to eat and needed a meal. Once my future husband, Henry, came as our Shabbos guest—he was in yeshiva in Sosnowiec and needed a place to eat. I didn't remember him when I met him later on because I was young at the time and wasn't paying attention.

My mother cared about people and was always trying to do good things and help. She made food for families when they had a baby or were sitting shiva. Once on Rosh Hashanah, our shul was crowded because everyone went, even the girls and little kids. There weren't enough chairs and some people couldn't afford to buy tickets. My mother sent me home to bring chairs from our house and I carried them back on my head. Some workers

---

[4] Cholent is a stew made from grated potatoes with meat and beans that needs to cook overnight and is traditionally eaten for lunch on Shabbos.

on the train tracks teased me and I was embarrassed.

We were very close to our Polish maid Marisha who was with us a long time. She went home to her village on Sunday mornings and came back in the evening. She invited us to visit her family at times, but we never went. I think we were nervous to show the other Polish people how close we were to Marisha.

There were no washing machines in those days. We washed our clothes by hand, using a big wooden barrel, and a special woman came three days a week to do our laundry. We used a dressmaker to make our clothes and she came to the house to fit us. We never bought ready-made shoes. Our shoes came from a shoemaker; one man cut the leather for the shoes and the other one would sew the leather and soles together.

We all went to yeshiva and Jewish public school (gymnasia). You were supposed to start school at seven years old, but I started a year early. Every day I walked with my mother and sister Vida Malka to school on Dęblińska Street and cried that I wanted to go also. Finally, my mother begged the school, "Take her to school because I can't take her crying anymore. If she's no good, throw her out," and they agreed.

I started school a year early and somehow, they put me a grade ahead. I went to school up until seventh grade when the war broke out. There were only girls in my school because it was a Bais Yaakov. We wore a black smock with a big white collar over our regular clothing. The secular subjects were taught in Polish. There were no Hebrew/Jewish subjects except for Jewish history. We davened and learned some Torah. I was very good at math and it was my favorite subject. What I really loved was gymnastics, which we had twice a week for an hour.

## Our Store

Our family owned a general store that sold household items and tools, and the store was attached to our first-floor apartment. The entrance was on the corner of Piłsudska and Składowa Streets. This was the European way, that your business was connected to your home. My parents worked long hours.

Our store opened very early in the morning because our customers worked in the coal mines and iron factories and their day started early. My father went to the wholesale bakery called "Dzewo" at around 5:00 a.m. to get bread for them to buy for their lunch sandwiches. We had all kinds of customers from the neighborhood—Jews, Christians, Poles, Germans, and even Gypsies.

The Gypsies stole things like beans, rice, and barley while we were measuring their order. We had to watch them carefully and let them know we were watching them. The Gypsies also had a reputation for kidnapping children, especially Jewish children, and even more so, Jewish girls. My parents warned us to watch the little kids carefully and keep them close when the Gypsies came to shop. My parents even watched me carefully because they were afraid that I would be taken. The Gypsies told my mother that I was a stolen Gypsy child because of my dark hair and dark eyes!

We stocked all kinds of food in the store. We sold flour, sugar, rice, beans, barley, tea, coffee, yeast, and other dry groceries, and even herring. These were delivered in huge boxes or sacks and we had to measure and weigh each item in decos or kilos in the amounts the customers asked for. One time, I found an American quarter as I was measuring tea from a large Wissotzky tea sack. I held on to that coin for a long time, until the Nazis took it away from me years later.

In addition, we sold pots and pans and recoppered the bottom of the frying pans. We had millstones for grinding corn into flour, scythes for cutting wheat, and other tools. We sold petroleum lamps with cotton wicks and glass globes for home use and special lamps encased in metal for the coal miners.

My mother worked alongside my father in the store. It was usual for women to work and help their husbands in their businesses, at least in Sosnowiec. My mother was a very good saleslady; she was warm and had close relationships with many of our customers who were not Jewish. Those close relationships helped us or tried to help us later when the Nazis took over.

I often worked in the store, unpacking the merchandise wrapped in wool. It was difficult to unpack the things and I did it very carefully. Sometimes, my younger sister, Estusha, who was four years younger, would also help. Afterward, we danced around and played with the wool. As I got older, I watched the store so my parents could eat supper. I was good at weighing and figuring out numbers, so they let me. In the store, I had to speak Polish to the customers, even sometimes German. That's why I spoke a very good Polish and my German became more fluent.

Sometimes, I helped my uncle Shimon Baer, who had a wholesale business of feed for cows and other animals. I used to cut hay on his farm and his worker farmers couldn't believe that such a young girl could cut hay like me. I loved doing it and being outdoors. Shimon Baer was my favorite uncle and he always teased my parents that they should give me to him because he and his wife didn't have children. He would say to my mother, "You have six kids. Why don't you give me Mira? She would be good for my business."

We got our news mostly from newspapers. There were Jewish newspapers and Polish newspapers. We had a radio and enjoyed listening to Jewish music programs. Telephones were rare but sometimes they were used for business purposes. No one had a car; we used the streetcars/trolleys or walked. Some people used bicycles.

## Growing Up

When I was thirteen, I was still too young to belong to any of the Jewish youth clubs like my older brothers. I started to hang out with friends and do things outside the neighborhood. I looked older than my age because I was very tall, about five foot seven, and many of my friends were two or three years older than I was. My parents weren't always comfortable with how much freedom I wanted. I loved going to the movies at Theatre Yoseph. You had to be sixteen to buy a ticket, which cost twenty-five cents, but I was so tall that no one checked me. My friends who were older needed papers to prove they were sixteen. The last movie I remember playing in the movie theater was Gone with the Wind but I can't remember if I saw it or not.

The most famous man from our neighborhood was Jan Kiepura, a famous Polish singer and actor who was married to the actress Marta Eggerth. They moved to Los Angeles but came back to Sosnowiec to visit his parents, who owned a small bakery. My parents and his parents were friends, and Jan was very friendly to me. When I was a little girl, he would put me on his knees and throw me in the air like a football. I had big dark eyes, and Jan teased me by saying that my eyes were dirty from the coal mines and told me that my mother had to wash them out to clean them. On one visit, Jan brought me a present from America—my first lipstick.

Jan's parents struggled to make a living and they borrowed money from my parents. His mother would swim across the Czarna Przemsza River into Germany and bring back bone-handled flatware to sell in Sosnowiec. This way, the family earned some extra money and eventually paid back my parents. When my parents began to seriously think about ways to get their children out of Poland before the war, they actually thought of asking Jan Kiepura to sponsor me for an American visa but nothing came of it. Much later, when I emigrated to America, I didn't contact Jan and ask for his help, but I should have.

# CHAPTER 2

# THE LENCZYCKI FAMILY IN SOSNOWIEC

## My Aunts and Uncles

My life was filled with much love and a feeling of belonging and security. Sosnowiec and the nearby towns were filled with my cousins and their families and we were together all the time—the Himmelfarbs, the Abramowiczes, and many others. We were a family of eight Rosenblatts surrounded by the larger Lenczycki family—all of my mother's brothers and sisters and their families who lived in Sosnowiec. I grew up living in the same house with my aunts and uncles and saw them grow up, get married, and have families. They were a big part of my life and I was lucky to have had this close extended family. I wanted to give an understanding of my warm, protected, and loving childhood and all that I lost because of the Holocaust. I was close to each and every one—all my aunts and uncles and their families, and I have tried to honor their lives by sharing my memories of them.

My mother was the eldest of nine siblings. The names of my mother's sisters and brothers in birth order were Shimon Baer, Rushka, Shaya, Moniek,

Franya, Chamech, Henia, and Abram.

**Shimon Baer Lenczycki** was married to **Frieda/Franya Wodzislaw** and they had no children. He had a successful wholesale and retail business selling hay and oats for the cows to farmers. The business was on the outskirts of the city located on Sienkiewicza Street. Shimon Baer was my favorite uncle and I spent a lot of time with him. He loved me also and always joked with my mother that she should give me to him. I spent a lot of time with him and used to go to his farm to cut hay and hang out in the countryside and play outside. Many times, I met my other aunts and uncles, who would visit and have something to eat and drink at a big table under the trees.

When the war started, Shimon Baer first ran to Warsaw, which was a terrible place to be. He bribed someone to smuggle Frieda and himself to Lvov (Lemberg) near the Russian border. In 1941, when the Germans declared war on Russia, they had to move again. They decided to go to Frieda's hometown of Wodzisław, near Kielce, to join her family. Frieda was finally pregnant after fifteen years of marriage and gave birth to a baby boy. They named him Mordechai Wolf. They waited so long to have a baby, but their joy was short-lived. A Polish neighbor reported the whole family to the Gestapo, who arrested them. There were many Jews arrested at this time, and during the confusion Shimon Baer jumped out of the window and escaped to the nearby city of Pilica, ultimately Shimon Baer did not survive. Frieda's brother also tried to escape but the SS guards caught him and set their dogs on him and they ripped him to death. The rest of the group of Jews, including Frieda and the baby, were marched through town to the Umschlagplatz. Frieda decided to give her baby a chance of survival and left Mordechai wrapped in a blanket in the marketplace as they passed through it. She hoped someone would find him and save him, that there still was someone alive with kindness left in the world. Frieda was deported to Ravensbruck concentration camp and gassed to death and the baby was left in the market.

I learned all these details from Chaim Wasserman from Pilica who was in my forced labor camp at Grünberg. I heard Chaim survived the war but I never saw him afterward. I tried to find the baby Mordechai after the war but was unsuccessful. I went back to the town twice to search for him, and my uncle Abram also went separately to search, but we were never able to find out any information about what had happened to the baby.

**Rushka Lenczycki** was married to **Leon Glicksman** from Lodz and they had two children named Helusha, born 1933, and Mietush, born 1935. They were wealthy and lived in a nice house on Modrzejowska 1 Street, the first house on the corner. Their house was large and many family events took place there. They had a maid, a governess for the children, and a large white dog. Leon was a banker and they owned three fancy stores that made expensive men's suits in English fabrics. Two stores were in Germany and one was in Sosnowiec. They were out of the country on vacation when the war broke out. They returned and lived in their apartment until Sosnowiec was made Judenrein. My aunt Rushka once told me that she would survive everything because they had a lot of money. They did survive many Aktions (Deportations) in Sosnowiec. In 1943, they were resettled into the Srodula ghetto along with the rest of the Jews from Sosnowiec. By the end of 1943, Rushka and her family were deported to Auschwitz and gassed to death.

**Franya Lenczycki** was married to **Alter Garfinkel** and they had one little girl, Helusha. They had an apartment in Targowa 21 Street, which was owned by my grandfather. They had a little coffee shop with pastries right by their apartment. The business wasn't successful, and they struggled financially. My aunt Franya was a beautiful woman and very nice to me. Alter was my first uncle to be arrested and deported to an arbeitslager (workcamp) by the Nazis in early 1940. Uncle Alter went outside one night to use the toilet in the courtyard and got caught in a raid by the Nazis and arrested. He was deported to Miloszyce, a labor camp that was part of Gross-Rosen concentration camps. His job was to carry big, heavy sacks of cement for twelve hours a day. Alter was a broad, healthy man but he collapsed and died soon after his arrest. My family learned about Uncle Alter's death from a friend of ours, Tadek Steinmetz, who was connected to both the Judenrat and the Gestapo in Sosnowiec.

Franya was pregnant with her second child and she and her little girl Helusha moved into our apartment when Alter was taken. In 1940, Franya gave birth to a baby boy, Meitush, in our dining room and I had to help with the delivery. I held her legs down while she pushed the baby out. I was so scared and never forgot her screams of childbirth. Franya never recovered from the difficult birth and Alter's death and could barely take care of her children. We all chipped in to help, and her two children were like my baby sister and brother. Franya died in the summer of 1942, shortly before the Great Aktion of August 12. Meitush was around two years old and Helusha was four years old when their mother died. They were hidden in a coal shed and escaped the Great Aktion and were resettled with my youngest siblings, Estusha and Natan, in the Srodula ghetto early in 1943. Before the end of 1943, all of them were deported to Auschwitz and gassed to death.

**Moniek Lenczycki** was married to **Lodja Goldman** from Furth, Germany, and they had one little boy named Jurek. She was related to the Goldman family of the American movie company and was wealthy. She often went by her maiden name, Lodja Goldman, rather than Lenczycki. Moniek was a tall, good-looking, athletic man. I remember that he was a great skier. Moniek was a committed Zionist, and in 1935 he emigrated to Palestine. He was a pioneer and wanted to take part in establishing a Jewish state. He worked in construction along with a cousin, Hanoch Rosenblatt. [5]

Moniek begged the whole family to apply for entry permits into Palestine and join him. He recommended that we go illegally if we couldn't get the visas. His wife, Lodja, refused to go unless she could enter Palestine legally, which was almost impossible. Moniek wasn't able to convince her and she wrote to him to "come back" and he did, returning to Poland late in 1938. By this time, anti-Semitism was terrible and war was inevitable. It was crazy that Moniek left the safety of Israel and returned to Poland. My mother and her brothers and sisters couldn't believe that Lodja had made Moniek come back and they were upset with her. It caused a strain in their relationship at a difficult time.

Moniek and Lodja and their young son Jurek lived in the older part of Sosnowiec in a very nice apartment across the street from a beautiful park

---

[5] Hanoch Rosenblatt was my father's cousin who made aliyah in the 1930s. He lived on Derech Maza in Tel Aviv and had five daughters. One of his daughters, Chana, married Manny Kozlowski, a young survivor who snuck into Israel on a boat (Aliyah Bet) after the war. They moved to America in the 1950s and we were close with them.

with benches and paths. It was near the sports stadium on Mireckiego Nova Aleja. We didn't see them often once the war started because they didn't live close by and Moniek kept himself hidden to protect himself and his family.

Moniek was a master at living in the shadows and was able to get by without working or being registered until the Great Aktion on August 12, 1942. He hid instead of reporting to the stadium but was discovered by the SS in their sweep two days later. Moniek was brought directly to the Dulag and shipped out to an arbeitslager, and from there to a concentration camp. I can't be sure which one but I think it was Auschwitz. I heard this from Moniek Purow, a member of the Judenrat when I was in the Dulag awaiting my deportation. [6]

Moniek's little boy Jurek must have been taken at the same time because his name appeared in Yad Vashem The Central Database of Shoah Victims' Names. List of Children Who Perished in the Holocaust, p. 148. He was listed as "Jurek Lenczycki b. 1932 Sosnowiec d. Auschwitz 1942." Lodja somehow remained in hiding throughout the war in Sosnowiec and survived. She promised people money and fame because of her connections to the Goldman family of films and this way she was protected.

After the war, Lodja lived in the family apartment building and was listed as #731 Leczycka Laja, b. 1903, at Targowa 21, 1946 in the Arolsen Archive, List of Jewish People Who Returned to Sosnowiec. [7] She moved to Furth, Germany and put up a memorial for my uncle Moniek and Jurek in the Jewish cemetery there. Lodja remarried a fellow survivor, Mr. Katz, who had been the matchmaker for her and my uncle Moniek many years earlier. Lodja decided to emigrate to Israel with her second husband after refusing to listen to my uncle's pleas before the war. The move didn't work out and after a short time, they returned to Furth where she lived for the rest of her life.

**Shaya Lenczycki** was married to **Helcha Lenczycki** [8] from Lodz and

---

[6] Moniek Purow was older, about thirty, and interested in me, but not in a nice way. He wanted to live and enjoy whatever he could. He said, "They are going to kill all of us anyways. Let's enjoy ourselves now." I was disgusted by him and his sexual suggestions.

[7] Arolsen Archives https://collections.arolsen-archives.org/en/search/topics/3-1-1-1_691000/?p=1&s=Sosnowiec&s_signature, title=asc, 403, p. 21. Arolsen Archives – International Center on Nazi Persecution, formerly known as the International Tracing Service

[8] Helcha was the daughter of my grandfather Mordechai Wolf's brother Hannoch

they had two children, Sabinka and Meitush. Shaya and Helcha shared the same grandparents and were cousins. It was common for cousins to marry in the Jewish communities in Poland. They lived in my grandfather's apartment building on Targowa 21. Shaya had a successful business manufacturing sofas and chairs that he sold all over Europe. Shaya and Helcha and their two little children were on summer vacation in Lodz when the war broke out. Shaya was able to return to Sosnowiec but Helcha and her children got stuck in Lodz when the Jews were moved into the ghetto in the early days of the war. It took a lot of effort, but Shaya was able to get his family out of the Lodz ghetto because of his connections. Shaya and Helcha returned to their apartment in Targowa 21 where my family now lived because we had been forced to move from our home. I saw my uncle Shaya and aunt Helcha every day and played with their kids, Sabinka and Meitush.

The Nazis seized Shaya's factory along with most other Jewish businesses in the first weeks of the war. They saw him as a skilled artisan and made him continue to manufacture and manage the workers in the factory. He had a special status as a necessary worker because of his skills and received decent rations. Shaya tried to share and helped the other family members when he could.

Shaya and his family marched to the stadium as ordered along with all the other Jews of Sosnowiec on August 12, 1942. Once they reached the stadium, Shaya was separated from Helcha and the two children. Shaya was "selected" as an essential worker and allowed to return home; Helcha, Sabinka, and Meitush were "selected" as nonessential workers and were sent to the Dulag. From there they were deported to either Ravensbruck or Auschwitz concentration camps and gassed to death.

By early 1943, Shaya had completed all of the outstanding orders for sofas and was no longer considered an essential worker. At this time, Sosnowiec was being Judenrein and all the Jews were relocated to the Srodula ghetto. Shaya was arrested and deported directly to a concentration camp and gassed

---

Lenczycki. Their little girl, Sabinka, was named for the mother of her father and uncle. Helcha's two brothers were Simon and Abram Lenczycki, who survived and moved to Australia. Simon and I were best of friends and he visited me in America often. I remained close with his children and grandchildren—Marilyn and Mishka, Talia and Stephanie.

to death. I thought it was Auschwitz, but I never knew for sure.

**Chamech Lenczycki** was married to **Baila/Baltsha** and they had one little girl named Helusha. They lived in nearby Będzin, which was considered to be part of greater Sosnowiec. Chamech and Baltsha were a little less religious than the other aunts and uncles. It was interesting that they lived in Będzin because it was a more religious city than Sosnowiec and had many big yeshivas. In 1940, Chamech was arrested in Będzin and put on a train to a labor camp. He jumped off the moving train and snuck into Sosnowiec. We were able to get word to his wife, Baltsha, and she and her daughter snuck out of Będzin and were reunited with Chamech. The whole family moved into our apartment.

Chamech and Baltsha decided to hide rather than report to the stadium on August 12, 1942. They heard the rumors of a new big Aktion and went into hiding a few days before August 12. The Nazis searched relentlessly for any Jews who were hiding and used dogs to help them search. Eventually, they found Chamech, Baltsha, and Helusha. They were taken directly to the deportation center at Targowa 4. Targowa 4 was another deportation center that used trucks to ship Jews out. Sometimes there weren't enough trains to deport all the Jews and the Nazis used whatever they could to transport the Jews to concentration camps. Chamech, Baltsha, and Helusha were all deported to Auschwitz concentration camp and gassed to death.

**Henia Lenczycki** was married to **Henrik Manela** and they had a little boy named Meitush. They had an optic store on Warszawska 10 Street near the movie theater in the center of town. They lived in the new part of Sienkiewicza Street near Koscielna Street, past the big church in town. It was at the exact opposite end of the street where my uncle Shimon Baer lived. Henia was beautiful and elegant and was more like an older sister than an aunt. I have clear memories of her engagement party and wedding, and I remember when their little boy, Meitush, was born. Henia and Henrick were very much in love and I have photographs from their courtship and as a young married couple that showed how happy they were. She was so young, only twenty-seven years old when the war started.

Henia and her family did not survive the Holocaust. A woman who worked with me at the Held factory told me that Henia and her family had been caught up in a big Aktion in their neighborhood in the spring of 1942. One of the SS guards told Henia to put down her baby and save herself. She did not abandon her baby boy, Meitush, but somehow Henia, Henrik, and the baby were able to escape that roundup and went into hiding. Perhaps they were helped by the SS guard or one of the priests or nuns in the big church by their apartment. We didn't see them after this Aktion—I remember hearing that they were too afraid to come to my aunt Franya's funeral. Years later, I found their three names with their matching birthdates and address on an official relocation list of Jews to the Srodula ghetto between February 17 and 22, 1943. Henia, Henrik, and Mordechai Manela are listed as #317 Henrik (Chaim Israel) born December 30, 1904; #318 Henia (Chaja Sara) born April 20, 1913; and #319 Mordechaj Isr. born April 8, 1939. [9] I never knew for certain what happened to the three of them, but I think they were probably deported to Auschwitz and gassed to death when Srodula was liquidated.

The names Meitush and Helusha were used over and over again. It was our custom to name children after our parents and grandparents who had died. It was a way of honoring their memory. Meitush or Mordechai was named after my grandfather Mordechai Wolf and Helusha was named after my great-grandmother who my mother was named for. All of my aunts and uncles chose to name their first girls after their grandmother because their mother, Baila Yehudis, was still alive when their daughters were born. Unfortunately, none of the children who were named so lovingly after my grandparents survived the Holocaust.

**Abram Lenczycki** (Lenn) was my youngest uncle and he was a rebel. Abram was a Communist and wasn't religious at all. He wore a cap out of respect for his family. Abram was in his early twenties and wasn't married. He was all alone because his parents, my grandparents, were dead. He went into hiding immediately when the war broke out and was never arrested,

---

[9] "Verzeichnie No. 10 der Juden, welche aus dem Bereucg des II. Pol. Rev. nach dem III. Pol. Rev./ Schrodel/in der zeir vom: 17-22.2.43. Doersiedelt wurde," p. 160. Number 34 of these documents, List No. 34, lists #152 and #153.

unlike my brothers on those first days of the war. Abram quickly ran away to Russia with Bella, a woman from Będzin. When I accompanied my older brothers to Lvov, I heard that my uncle Abram had escaped into Russia and made it to Siberia.

Abram was the only one of all nine siblings who survived the Holocaust. He came back to Sosnowiec, but by then I was living in Germany. Abram married a woman named Genia Abman from Lodz after the war and they had two girls, Helena and Mariola. He remained in Sosnowiec and was a government bureaucrat under the Soviet regime until the anti-Semitic purges in 1956–1957. Abram and his family then fled to Germany and had to wait for three years to receive their emigration papers to America because of his Communist background. In 1961, he joined my brother Herschel and myself in Springfield, Massachusetts.

# CHAPTER 3

# PREWAR YEARS: 1934–1939

## Life Begins to Change: 1934

My grandparents were a big part of my childhood and I loved them very much. We lived in the same building and I saw them every day. My zaide struggled with asthma and died around 1934. My bubbe got sick soon after and my mother stayed with her in the big hospital in Krakow. Marisha took care of the household during this time. My bubbe didn't get better and died in 1934. Everything seemed to change with their deaths. Life began to feel different and my happy childhood was nearing an end.

I was sad about my zaide and bubbe and the whole family was in mourning. I have memories of walking with my mother to the cemetery when she visited her parents' graves. It was a time of great uncertainty for me as a child. Yet, in retrospect, I am so relieved that my grandparents never experienced or knew what their children and grandchildren went through after their deaths.

In 1935, soon after my grandparents died, Josef Piłsudski, the Polish leader, died. It became a time of great insecurity for all the Jews in Poland because Piłsudski had treated the Jews decently. The Polish people used to say that the "Jewish grandfather had died." With his death, I began to be aware that life was more difficult not for just for my family but for all the Jews in Poland.

My grandfather sold the apartment building on Piłsudska 61 right before he died, and we became tenants with no special privileges. I didn't know why he sold it—perhaps because of the growing pressure on Jews not to own property. We still had the store. My aunts and uncles didn't live in the building anymore because they were now married and had moved to the new part of Sosnowiec.

Stary Sosnowiec, where I lived, was considered the older part of Sosnowiec and was closer to the coal mines and farms on the outskirts of the city. Our neighborhood was made up of working-class Polish people and many Volksdeutsch, some Gypsies, as well as Jews. They were all our customers and shopped in our store. Volksdeutsch were half-German Poles who lived in our area because of our closeness to Germany. They believed in the Nazi propaganda and started to act to the Jews as if Poland was Germany. The anti-Jewish laws and activities in Germany spilled over into our neighborhood and there were more and more anti-Semitic incidents. It was disturbing and even scary. [10]

## No Longer a Child: 1937

By 1937 our lives had changed dramatically. We still had a normal family life but every month it seemed harder to keep it going. Sometimes it was difficult to walk down the street in our area. Random people threw stones, broke the windows in our store, and sometimes beat up Jews in passing. This was

---

[10] Per Jeff Cymbler of the Będzin-Sosnowiec-Zawiercie Area Research Society: "'Police End Blockade of Jewish Stores,' Sosnowiec, July 1936: Youthful anti-Semites in this town organized a vigilance committee which systematically prevented persons from entering Jewish stores. . . ." "'Boy Injured by a Bomb: In Anti-Semitic Rioting—Jewish Store Windows Broken,' Sosnowiec, November 17, 1935: A fourteen-year-old boy was reported near death today in Sosnowiec as the result of a bomb thrown into a Jewish house of prayer. The incident was one of a number in an anti-Semitic outbreaks over the weekend."

happening long before Kristallnacht in November 1938.

It was no longer safe for my father to go to the bakery alone early in the morning, so I went with him. There were all kinds of restrictions and you had to be careful about everything you did. Jews couldn't wear fur coats because the Volksdeutsch threw petroleum on you and then tried to set you on fire. After you paid the taxes on the buildings, the taxes would be raised. Everything was complicated and changing around us.

We had a neighbor who owned a similar business to ours, Mrs. Kornfeld, but I also knew her as Mrs. Zambrani. She was a vicious, crude woman who spoke to her husband as if he were a dog—"whoever she could bite, she bit; whoever she could harm, she did." She was always trying to get us into trouble with the authorities. She reported that we sold merchandise secretly on Sundays, which wasn't allowed. Jews weren't allowed to own fur coats anymore and she told the authorities about my father's coat that was lined in fur. Mrs. Kornfeld/Zambrani once got in a fight with my father and she attacked him and ripped out hair from his beard. Everyone was disgusted by her—even our Polish neighbors. She used to call me "pisher" and was always rude and mean to me. Somehow, Mrs. Kornfeld ended up working at the same factory in the ghetto as me and later at my labor camp. She continued to cause trouble for me whenever she could.

The Volksdeutsch told the Poles not to buy from the Jews and began an unofficial campaign to boycott all Jewish stores. Our store was hurt right away, and business got bad. We had loyal customers but one by one they stopped shopping by us. One of the nuns, Mother Teresa Kierocinska, from the convent across the street on 25 Wiejska, came to my mother, kissed her hand, and said, "I cannot talk to Jews and I cannot come here anymore." [11]

After Kristallnacht—the Night of Broken Glass, in November 1938—the boycott of Jewish stores was so strong that even our most loyal customers were afraid to shop by us. The Gypsies ran away and the Volksdeutsch actively boycotted us. We closed the store soon afterward but continued to

---

[11] Convent of Carmelite Sisters of Infant Jesus, https://sprawiedliwi.org.pl/en/stories-of-rescue/story-rescue-kierocinska-janina.

live in our apartment on Piłsudska Street. Life changed for all of us in big and small ways.

I was a tough cookie and always stood up for myself. I didn't let anyone take advantage of me or let anyone get bullied when I was around. All the neighbor kids played all kinds of games together. Jump rope was one of our favorite games but sometimes the boys played rough and twirled the rope to hit the girls in the neck. One time, they hit a girl hard and I took those two punks and pushed them into the coal shed and locked them in for two hours. I warned them if they did it again, I would lock them in overnight.

Sometimes the smallest things were the hardest to take. A nice neighbor and good friend of the family had given me a pretty salamander pin as a present. I loved it and wore it on my coat. Things between Jews and non-Jews were bad, but the neighborhood kids still played together. That day, the Polish boys yanked the salamander pin off my coat and ran away with it. A year earlier, I would have run after them, hit them, and grabbed my pin back. I stood frozen and humiliated because I realized that I couldn't do that anymore. I was no longer free to stand up for myself.

My parents began to think of ways for us to leave Poland or try to keep us safe. Some of our customers from the store tried to help. My parents discussed the possibility of me moving to Australia to a cousin who was a dressmaker. My mother decided I should learn to sew before I moved so I could help my cousin. She arranged for me to work with a noted dressmaker, Marycia Goldberg, who made fancy gowns for actresses. One time, Mrs. Goldberg gave me one of the gowns, which I later sold when we needed money, even before the war started. Nothing came of the plan for me to move to Australia, but knowing how to sew and iron helped me during the war.

The nice Polish neighbor who gave me the salamander pin was very close to my family. She was a special lady and I wish I could remember her name, but I remember that she lived on Dęblińska 5 Street. She used her extra ration cards to buy us eggs and other food when she could. This courageous woman offered to hide Estusha and me. She had a perfect place; under her bed was a door that led to a subbasement with no windows and no other access. My mother seriously considered her offer, but it was too late. The woman's son-in-law got involved with the Nazis and it became too risky.

My mother Helena Lencyzcki Rosenblatt, 1925 (taken at Zorski Studio on Modrzejowsko Street)

My parents Helena and Shlomo Yitzhak with baby Vida Malka, Manek standing and Herschel sitting, Sosnowiec 1921

My father, Shlomo Yitzhak 1938

My brother Herschel in his HaPoel Mizrachi uniform, 1938

My brother Manek, c.1937

My brother Herschel with friends, Sosnowiec 1938. L to R: Poznanski (survived, Nice, Italy); Skopicki (survived, San Jose, California); my brother Herschel; Szpira (died in Holocaust); Adler (died in Holocaust)

My grandmother's Baila Yehudis Abramowicz unveiling in the Old Cemetery in Sosnowiec, January 22, 1935. L to R: my Uncle Chamech Lenczycki; my mother Helena Rosenblatt; my Aunt Rushka Glicksman; my Aunt Helcha Lenczycki; my Aunt Frieda Lenczycki; my Aunt Henia. Other side of gravestone: my Aunt Franya Garfinkel; my Uncle Shaya Lenczycki; my Uncle Shimon Baer Lenczycki; Rabbi Abramowicz, my great uncle and brother of Baila Yehudis; my Uncle Abram Lenczycki; my Aunt Lodja Lenczycki; my Uncle Alter Garfinkel. [My Uncle Moniek Lenczycki is missing; I believe he was in Palestine/Israel]

My aunts and uncles on vacation, Krynica, CZ, c. 1935/36. L to R: Leon Glicksman; Frieda and Herschel Himmelfarb; Shimon Baer without a shirt; Rushka; Henia

My Uncle Shimon Baer's house, 1930s. L to R: Shimon Baer in white pants; cousin Frieda; Rushka and Leon Glicksman

My Aunt Rushka with her children, Helusha and Mietus, resort town of Szesawnica, Poland c. 1935

My Aunt Rushka with her children Helusha and Mietus,
Wakacjon, Sosnowiec c. 1936/37

My Aunt Rushka's children, Helusha and Mietus Glicksman,
c. 1936

My Aunt Freida, wife of my Uncle Shimon Baer, c. 1935

My Aunt Lodja Goldman, wife of my Uncle Moniek, 1945

My Uncle Shaya's wife Helcha and their children, Sabinka and Mietus and nanny, Lodz 1937. Helcha was the sister of Simon from Australia.

Engagement picture of my Aunt Henia to Henrik Manela, Sosnowiec October 1936

Engagement party of my Aunt Henia Lenczycki and Henrik Manela, 1936/37. Standing L to R: my brother Manek; my Uncle Shimon Baer Lenczycki with glasses; my brother Herschel; Romek who worked in their optic store; my Uncle Chamech Lenczycki; Henrik's sister; Henrik's second sister; the 'kallah' Henia in the print shirt; my Aunt Franya Garfinkel; my Uncle Moniek Lenczycki. Seated L to R: Rabbi Manela, father of Henrik; my Uncle Leon Glicksman; the 'chossen' Henrik Manela; unnamed friend; my Aunt Frieda Lenczycki; my Aunt Rushka Glicksman

My Aunt Henia and Uncle Henrik Manela in their optic store, Sosnowiec 1938

My Aunt Henia Lenczycki Manela with her baby Mietus, Sosnowiec 1940

Family get together with cousins Himmelfarb and Abramowicz, Sosnowiec 1938. Gutsha Himmelfarb standing in light sweater, third from left is the only person who survived the Holocaust. Seated on the bottom left are my aunts Rushka and Henia (with white collar).

## CHAPTER 4

# WORLD WAR II IN SOSNOWIEC: SEPTEMBER 1, 1939–AUGUST 12, 1942

### World War II Begins: September 1, 1939

The Germans invaded Poland on Friday, September 1, 1939, and World War II began. By Monday, September 4, 1939, the Germans occupied Sosnowiec. I was sixteen years old and my life as I knew it was over. In my worst nightmares, I had no idea what the next six years would be like. Life had been difficult ever since the Nazis came to power in 1933. Every year I saw changes that limited our personal freedom and livelihood. Every year we became more anxious and fearful. Yet, we were totally unprepared for the devastation that was to come now that the war had started.

The Germans victoriously rode their motorcycles into Sosnowiec at 1:30 p.m. on that Monday. The Einsatzgruppe and SS divisions took immediate and brutal control of the city and all the Jews. We hid in our homes and listened to the Germans on their loudspeakers screaming out orders and heard the gunshots as they shot anyone who was in their way. When we peeked out the windows, we saw dead people lying all over the streets. By 6:00 p.m., the Germans arrested all males sixteen years and older and took them away. My father and my two older brothers, Herschel and Manek, were taken on that first day. Anyone who resisted was lying dead in the street.

After my father and brothers were taken, we waited inside to see what was going to happen next. We were still living on Piłsudska 64 Street. The next day was calmer, with less shooting and fewer orders being shouted out. A neighbor came over and told my mother that she had heard that my father had been shot and was dead. I was young and headstrong and curious about what was going on outside. I wanted to see the situation for myself. I left the house to find out if the neighbor was correct and to see if my brothers were still alive. The streets were filled with dead people still lying where they had been shot or beaten to death. I went from body to body, picking up the heads of each person to check to see if one of them was my father. I didn't find him.

I heard noises and followed the sound to the City Hall garage where the Nazis had locked up all the arrested men. They were torturing them by pouring cold water from large hoses all over them. I couldn't get close enough to see if my father and brothers were inside. Other people had also come to look for their family members. I asked someone if they had seen my family and they told me, "Yes, your brothers and father are here." It was a hot day and the Nazis allowed us to bring water for the locked-up men to drink. We ran to fill up containers with water but when we came back with them, the Nazis spilled out the water and laughed at us.

I saw my cousin and asked him and some of the people standing around what we could do to get the men out; maybe there was a way we could try to buy them out. They didn't know what to do and had no answers. One man said he would try to get them out. This man was Moshe Merin, who became the head of the Judenrat and was in charge of the Jewish community in Sosnowiec for the Nazis. [12]

---

[12] In January 1940, Moshe Merin became the Head of the Jewish Council of Elders of Eastern Upper Silesia. At this point, the community of Jews amounted to almost one hundred thousand members. Merin actively promoted his major concept of "survival by work." He believed that only working for the Third Reich combined with obedience and subordination

The Nazis moved the men to the main square near Maja 3 Street where there was a large old factory, formerly the Szajn factory. Here, they began to torture the Jews—beating them up, humiliating them, ripping out their beards, etc. I finally saw my father—it was terrible. His beard had been ripped out and his teeth were knocked out. He had holes in his skin and was bleeding. He looked completely changed. Later he had his teeth fixed, but his face remained deformed because the holes never closed up. I couldn't get him out because he was still arrested, but at least I knew he was alive. It was nighttime and it was a problem for me to get home because Jews were no longer allowed to walk on Piłsudska Street. Two other girls and I finally made it back home using the side streets.

The Germans separated the men into groups and sent the young men to prison. It took two days to make up the groups. On the second day there was so much blood from the beatings and kicking. Some men were released because of bribes but most of the young men were sent to the prison at Towarowa Street. My father was finally released and came home wearing a scarf around his face to hide his wounds. My father was a changed man after this. He had been the strongest person I knew and now he was a broken person. My mother became more of the head of the household and had to make many of the decisions.

Meanwhile I was running around town trying to do things to help people, but things were happening too fast. In the evening of September 9 at 7:00 p.m., the Nazis blew up the Great Synagogue on Dekerta Street along with two other big shuls in Sosnowiec. A big crowd gathered to try to put out the fires and save the Torahs. I was with my friend Karol Tuchschneider who lived on the same street as the synagogue. We were part of a water brigade, filling up pails of water as fast as we could. The Germans threatened to arrest the whole group if we didn't leave immediately. Before they let us leave, the Nazis made us sweep the streets of the burned wood and ash. The Germans always wanted everything to be clean and neat.

---

toward the aggressor could guarantee Jewish survival. This policy caused objections, especially among Jewish youth involved in the resistance movement. "Moshe Merin: Savior, Collaborator or an Astray Man?" *Studia Judaica* 21, no. 42 (2018): 33; Central and Eastern European Online Library, https://www.ceeol.com/search/article-detail?id=789863.

Rabbi Englard, our rabbi, was sitting on the street crying and I took him along with some others through an alleyway to Targowa 21 Street, past the apartment building my grandparents had owned. Rosh Hashanah was a few days later, on September 14, but I don't remember it at all. Life had changed so much.

Herschel and Manek were taken to the prison in town. The Nazis had a rule that if one German was killed or hurt, ten Jews would be shot to death on the spot. The Nazis used to take ten men to dig a hole and then ten men went into the hole. Once Herschel was digging a hole and a guy he knew, Emanuel Himmelfarb, screamed out from the ground, "Hesiek, I am alive, help me." Herschel closed his ears and his eyes and kept shoveling but he never got over the horror of this. My brothers were released before November 11, which was Polish Independence Day.

The Nazis confiscated Jewish stores and homes and relocated us into specific areas of town that became the ghetto. They seized our building on Piłsudska 64 Street, kicked out all the Jews, and moved Germans into our apartments. They took everyone's furniture and possessions. [13]

## Leaving My Childhood Home: 1939

It was hard to leave my childhood home. I had never lived anywhere else. The German woman who moved into my home also took the skirt I was wearing that day. It was a pretty skirt, white with purple grapes on it, and she told me to give it to her. I couldn't believe it. I said to her, "What will I wear?

---

[13] A firsthand account documented by Shimon Huberband (1909–1942), an amateur historian and part of Emanuel Ringelblum's underground Oneg Shabbat archive. "On Monday night, September 4, 1939, German forces invaded Sosnowiec, a town on the road from Katowice to Będzin, about six kilometers (four miles) from the former. In 1939, the Jewish population was around twenty-eight thousand (21.5% of the total population)." According to Huberband (see his *Kiddush Hashem*, p. 287), "as soon as they entered the town, they arrested three hundred Jews, herded them into the Medical Insurance Building, and shot all three hundred of them that night. The next day all male Jews were interned in a camp within 'Schein's factory' where beards were shaved and the prisoners subjected to brutal torture . . ." (p. 137). Shimon Huberband, *Kiddush Hashem: Jewish Religious and Cultural Life in Poland During the Holocaust*, ed. Jeffrey Gurock and Robert Hirt (Hoboken, NJ: Ktav, 1987), p. 287, and included in Alexandra Garbarini, Emil Kerenji, Jan Lambertz, and Avinoam Patt, *Jewish Response to Persecution: 1938–1940* (Lanham, MD: AltaMira Press, 2011).

I can't leave in my panties." She gave me an old ragged skirt and took away my skirt like it was the most normal thing to do.

Our neighbor, Mr. Faselov, helped the Nazis steal our furniture. He was a tall, mean man who had a vicious dog that I was really afraid of. I told him that the Nazis had taken everything from us and begged him to give us back our furniture and things. He threw me out of his house two times, but finally he gave me back the furniture. It was already marked with swastikas as owned by the Germans. Mr. Faselov said, "This is the first time I did anything for a Jew." Later, he became friendlier and tried to help me when I had troubles.

I then sold our furniture to Mr. Loz, a German customer of my uncle Shaya, who owned a furniture store that made sofas. The Germans had already seized his factory. I sold our furniture because we needed the money more than we needed the furniture.

We left Piłsudska and moved to Targowa 21 Street, which was a forty two-tenant apartment building owned by my grandfather. It was two miles away from my old neighborhood, more in the center of the new part of Sosnowiec. We took over the apartment that my zaide had given to the Alexander Chassidim to use as their shtiebel (small synagogue). They were no longer allowed to use it so we moved in. The apartment was on the first floor of the building and faced the courtyard.

The apartment had two large rooms and, very importantly, two entrances. The main entrance was on Targowa Street and the other entrance led to two different streets—Warszawska and Glowaka Streets.

I slept with Vida Malka, Estusha, and Natan in the kitchen and my parents and brothers slept in the other room, which was also used as a dining room. Marisha, our Polish maid, moved in with us even though she wasn't allowed to work for Jews anymore. She had been with us for a long time and was very attached to my mother. She had to leave soon after our move; it was too dangerous for her to continue to stay with us. Before she left, Marisha pleaded with my mother to come with her and that she would hide all of us. My mother didn't think we would be safer in the countryside and refused her kind offer. She also thought we were too many people for Marisha to hide safely. Of course, we didn't know that in a month, my two older brothers would be gone and it would only be six of us. Maybe it would have worked out to have Marisha hide us in the countryside.

We were friends with many of the tenants in the building. I even remember many of their names: Neigerbauer; Praiser; Meller; Szyszcicki; Pariser; Kalin; Bankers; Wislenski; and of course my family; my aunt Franya and uncle Alter, my uncle Shaya and aunt Helcha, and later, my uncle Chamech and aunt Baltsha and all of their children.

The superintendent of the building was named Rogalski. He was a nice older man who tried to help us whenever he could. He had a kind heart and looked away from things that we did so as not to make our lives more miserable. He was kind to my aunt Franya and her children during her difficulties. I gave him my photographs for safekeeping, and I got them back after the war.

When the war broke out, some people were still away on summer vacation and never returned home. Others had been arrested immediately and taken away. There were empty apartments, but as more Jews were forcibly resettled into Sosnowiec, it became difficult to find a place to live.

We helped Rabbi Luzerie and his family from Oświęcim/Auschwitz get an apartment in Targowa 21. We tried to give them extra bread and food whenever we could because they had a hard time getting enough food. The Nazis had kicked out all the Jews from Oświęcim in the first days of the war and resettled them into Sosnowiec. This happened in many smaller towns, so there were a lot of people being relocated to the bigger city of Sosnowiec from different areas who needed places to live.

A German officer came to speak to my mother. It was an unbelievable scene when he came into our courtyard and took my mother's hand and kissed it. If the Nazis had seen this or someone had reported this to them, the German officer would have been in big trouble, even arrested. He had lived in Piłsudska 64 with us when the German army requisitioned the building during World War I and had remained close with my parents. He had gone back to Piłsudska Street, but we were no longer living there. It took him weeks to find us at Targowa Street, but he was determined to warn my mother of how dangerous the situation was. My mother took him inside and they talked seriously for a long time. He said, "Helena, take your kids and go away from this place, go as far away as you can go. Leave now." But it was already too late for us.

The Nazis quickly took control and made many laws. They arrested the richest Jews, seized their property, and held them for ransom for two weeks. They gave our homes to Germans who were ordered to move into our city by the Reich. We had to find work as forced laborers to get ration cards for food. By November, we had to wear white armbands with a blue Star of David. Before Christmas, the Nazis confiscated Jewish property, factories, stores, and houses. Later, around May 1941, our armbands were replaced with the yellow Jewish star with the word "Jude" that we wore on the front and back of our clothes. You needed permits to do everything; to walk on certain streets; to travel between towns: everything was controlled and restricted. You could be punished for almost anything. There were so many rules and they changed all the time. You never knew what would get you into trouble or get you beaten or arrested.

The Nazis turned the Jewish Business School in my old neighborhood into a transit center, the Umschlagplatz, where they deported the Jews to labor and concentration camps. The school had just opened and was barely used before the Nazis built wooden bunk beds in the classrooms and surrounded the courtyard with barbed wire. It became known as the Dulag.

We were able to get my brothers released before November with money through our connections with Moshe Merin. A few weeks after my brothers had been released, there were rumors that the Nazis were going to round up the young men again. The Germans were nervous about Polish Independence Day, which was November 11, and they planned to rearrest all the men again. We were warned about the impending arrests by a neighbor, Tadek Steinmetz. The SS came to our house to arrest them but my brothers slipped out the second hidden door in our apartment and escaped.

My parents decided that it would be safer if Herschel and Manek ran away to the Russian front and they wanted me to go with them. I went with them as far as Lvov (Lemberg) in the eastern part of Poland. There were many Jews fleeing to the Russian front and my brothers ran away with three close friends: Ocha, Skopitzki, and Skopitzki's girlfriend, Yadja. All five of them survived the war! I left the group and returned home when I heard that my mother had been arrested. This turned out to be false information, but I didn't really want to leave my parents anyway.

## Ghetto Life: 1940

The Nazis established a ghetto in Sosnowiec and all the Jews had to live within the boundaries. Our apartment was located within those boundaries, so we didn't have to move again. I worked in the Held factory, which was known as the Bigelie. The factory manufactured uniforms for soldiers and was part of the Schmelt Organization. [14] I got the job through Mr. Prizer, who lived in our building. He worked there before the war and was able to get jobs for Vida Malka and myself. I worked the night shift from 6:00 p.m. to 6:00 a.m. and my sister worked the day shift from 6:00 a.m. to 6:00 p.m. She worked on the buttonholes.

For two years, I ironed 120 shirts a day and had to fold them up "proper." It was considered elite, good work and my supervisor was Chaim Kuperminc, who was one of the Mizrachi leaders in Sosnowiec and involved with the Zionist underground groups against the Nazis. [15]

Ironing was hard in those days; you had to use coal to heat the iron and be very careful not to burn the shirts or burn yourself. There were two rooms, with three long tables and three people at each table. If you didn't do enough or do a good job, you were punished with no food rations. Mrs. Kornfeld/Zambrani worked in this factory alongside me and whenever she burned a shirt, she tried to blame me so she wouldn't lose her food rations.

Every morning, after I finished my shift, I met Estusha, my ten-year-old

---

[14] Organization Schmelt was a network of 177 labor camps under SS-Oberführer Albrecht Schmelt designated as "Special Representative of the Reichsführer SS for the Employment of Foreign Labor in Upper Silesia," headquartered in Sosnowiec. The Schmelt Organization and its work force was incorporated into the Gross Rosen Concentration Camp network. Every labor camp, factory, and concentration camp that Mira and Henry Rosenblatt were forced to work in were part of the Schmelt Organization from their very first days of the war to the very last day; even the subcamps of Auschwitz were part of the organization.

[15] Chaim Kuperminc and a number of Zionist resistance members were arrested in the spring of 1942 Aktion along with Rabbi Englard.

sister. Together we went to get food and find things to buy and sell on the black market because we needed money to buy more food. I didn't sleep much for the two years I worked ironing because there was no time. As a forced laborer, I had papers that allowed me to walk on any street. I hid merchandise under my clothing and snuck it out of the factory and then sold those things to bring in money to buy more food.

I also bought material from Olstein textile store, where my brother Herschel had worked, to sell on the black market. I had a big fight with Olstein because he charged me more than my wealthy aunt Rushka for goods. I told him it wasn't right because my sister Vida Malka and I were supporting our whole family on our two ration cards. Olstein then charged me less for the goods.

Lampel bakery was near our apartment on Targowa and I used to go there to get bread when I finished work. One time, two Nazis started up with me. They grabbed my loaf of bread and played a game of monkey in the middle with my precious loaf. When they tired of the game, they just walked away, taking my bread with them. I went back into the bakery and stole a loaf of bread, not something I am proud of, but I was desperate. After that, I always hid my loaf of bread under my coat and threw it into our courtyard. I'd walked around the corner and quickly picked up the bread when I got inside our courtyard. This way the Nazis couldn't take my bread from me, and later I wasn't even allowed this extra bread, so if the Nazis had found me with it, I would have been beaten up or arrested.

I was always willing to take risks. One of the riskiest things I did was to steal a German soldier's uniform from the factory where I worked. I gave it to my friend Karol Tuchschneider, who was a member of the Hanoar Hazioni, a Zionist group active in the underground. Karol snuck into Hungary wearing that uniform to warn the Jews there about what was going on in Poland. The people said, "We will report you to the police for spreading false stories." Karol made his way to Palestine/Israel while the war was still going on in Europe. [16]

---

[16] "Nasza Grupa" was a group of young Jews, mostly sixteen to twenty-five years old from the "Hanoar Hazioni" youth movement who gathered together in early 1942 in the

Sometimes I traveled outside of town to look for food. I took off my armband and put a scarf over my head to look like an old woman and walked two hours to the farms. I picked up these tiny potatoes that the farmers left in the fields because they were so small. We used these few small potatoes to make a soup that lasted for a few days. I learned about these little potatoes that the farmers left behind in the fields from our Gypsy customers.

My uncle Alter was the first person in the family to get arrested and deported. Early in 1940, he was sent to nearby Miłoszyce concentration camp, leaving his wife, my aunt Franya, pregnant and alone with her little girl Helusha. When Franya went into labor, my parents sent me to get the doctor. It was dangerous and difficult to get the doctor because many of the streets were forbidden for Jews to use. I had to circle around to find a safe route and it took a long time. The doctor came, which was very courageous, and then afterward I had to help him get back home. It was a very difficult birth and they needed my help. I didn't know which was more frightening, helping with the birth or getting the doctor.

Our apartment at Targowa 21 was filled with family. My aunt Franya and her two children and my uncle Chamech and aunt Baltsha and their little girl all lived with us. It was difficult to feed everyone because, although they were registered and received ration cards, they were allowed a limited amount of food as nonworkers. Vida Malka and I were the only two people who worked and received upgraded ration cards that let us get more food and walk in certain areas of the city. In addition, we needed to buy medicines for Franya, who was getting weaker.

In 1940, the Nazis were hunting down four girls who lived in our building. My mother helped the girls and hid them in the coal shed. The Nazis searched the area for them and ripped the locks off the shed and found the girls. My

---

Zaglembie region in northwest Poland. The group sabotaged German property, attempted to prevent the deportation of Jews to Auschwitz, obtained false documents for young Jewish men and women, and smuggled escaping Jews across borders. Approximately fifty members of the group survived. "Nasza Grupa" members Carol [Karol] Tuchschneider and Leon Blatt were in charge of smuggling people out of the ghetto. This group joined forces with "Hanoar Hatzair" in Hungary. They set up weapons, training camps, forged documents, traveled to peripheral areas to warn Jews of what was coming, "One for All" "Nasza Grupa" "Hanoar Hazioni" Underground in Zaglembie,
https://www.yadvashem.org/yv/en/exhibitions/rescue-by-jews/nasza-grupa.asp.

mother and the girls were arrested and taken a few miles away, past the neighboring town of Będzin, and put in jail there. The Nazis beat up my mother badly and forced her to work on the ground, digging and turning over the dirt for the farmers.

I found out where my mother was taken from the Jewish Gemeinde. I got a travel permit to go to her through the help of Tadek Steinmetz, who knew my family well. Tadek was known as a "Machor and a Kallamachor" (a Doer and a Destroyer), meaning he could help but sometimes his help made things worse. Tadek was Jewish and worked both sides; sometimes he helped Jews and other times he passed information to the Nazis. He was in this position because his former Polish maid spoke a perfect German and now worked for the Nazis. She passed information to him, and sometimes Tadek had to pass information back to her to give to the Nazis. Everything was so complicated in relationships and friendships. Tadek always helped me and he helped this time as well. He arranged for the travel permit and helped me get my mother released by paying money.

By the time I got to my mother, she was spitting up blood. I asked the Nazis to let me work instead of her. They said no. After two weeks, I was able to get her released and take her home. My mother was weak and sick from her hard labor, but she slowly recovered. The four girls were released and two of them survived the war. I met them afterward and later became good friends with one of their nieces, Ziesel, who was a jeweler in the Diamond District on Forty-seventh Street in New York City.

## Ghetto Life Continues . . .

In 1941, we were trying to survive with all the changing rules and legal papers needed for the Reich. There were permits for everything, for the kind of food you could buy, for clothes, for trolley trips, for riding a bicycle. The permits always needed to be updated and restamped. Everyone was running around trying to keep on top of the latest edicts and make sure they could still work, still live where they were, but it was nerve-racking. Vida Malka and I continued to work; my mother took care of Franya and her two children.

Every day was a struggle to feed everyone and there was always another new struggle and new heartache. The ration cards kept being downgraded, so we got to buy less and less food. Selling on the black market didn't work anymore—there were no goods to sell, and no one had money to buy them anyway. There seemed to be only bad news. We were a close-knit community and somehow information was passed along. Even though the information was always bad news, everyone wanted to know because it was your family, it was your loved ones.

Life was hard but we were together and still alive except for my uncle Alter. By 1942 things began to change rapidly. Often there were random raids and roundups in various neighborhoods without any specific reason. Jews were grabbed off the street and deported. There were also more formal Aktions where nonessential workers were ordered to report and then deported. Everyone knew that there were labor camps, which were horrible places where people sometimes died.

We began to hear rumors about something worse—concentration camps where you didn't get to work. I had heard the name Auschwitz by this time and was aware of the horrible reputation but really couldn't fully comprehend what it was. I can't remember if we knew anything about being gassed to death.

Right before Passover in 1942, the SS had an Aktion and emptied out all the Jews in Targowa 11 and Modrzejowska 2, which were two large buildings in the center of the ghetto. Rabbi Englard wore his tefillin on his arm and the *rosh* on his head and led the group as they were forcibly removed from their homes and put in the Theatre Yoseph until they were deported. I slipped into the theater to bring a sandwich for the rabbi to eat but he never ate it. In the meantime, I got stuck in the theater as more SS surrounded the building. Tadek Steinmetz came to my rescue again and put a Red Cross armband on me and took me out from the locked doors. The entire group walked through town later that day to the train station to be deported. Rabbi Englard was a "Gadol haDor" who my whole family held in the highest regard. I never can forget the image of Rabbi Englard being marched through the streets with the *rosh* from his tefillin on his forehead. [17]

My aunt Franya died in the summer of 1942. She was lucky; she died in her own bed and had a grave of her own. She was buried in the old Jewish cemetery where her parents were buried. We were responsible for her two little children who were now orphans. Something strange happened right before Franya died that was very spooky. It was traditional that family members came to ask forgiveness before someone died. My aunt Rushka came to Franya's deathbed to ask forgiveness and suddenly white foam came pouring out of Franya's mouth—Franya was already dead! Everyone was frightened and ran out of the room. People talked and said it happened because Rushka wasn't a good sister, but who really knew why.

Franya's funeral was our last family event because a few weeks later the Nazis implemented the Great Aktion and deported most of the Jews of Sosnowiec. My aunt Rushka and uncle Leon, my uncle Shaya and my aunt Helcha, my uncle Chamech and aunt Baltsha, my uncle Moniek and my aunt Lodja, and my parents were all at the cemetery. My aunt Henia and uncle Henrik were not there—I believe they were in hiding. My uncle Abram was in Russia, and no one had any idea of where my uncle Shimon Baer and aunt Frieda were.

[17] From amongst the five thousand Jews from Sosnowiec called to report for deportation on the tenth of May 1942, around three hundred came to the assembly point, and Jewish policemen were sent to search the houses. By the afternoon, the quota had not been reached, the Gestapo was enlisted to carry out searches. The SS men encircled three large buildings in Targowa Street, combed the apartments, and hauled out all the residents, among them Rabbi Englard and several other public figures like Chaim Kuperminc, one of the Mizrachi leaders in Sosnowiec. The Judenrat approached the Gestapo with a request to release them. However, their response was negative, with the excuse that the quota of deportees had yet to be met. On the eleventh of May, Meryn ordered his policemen and clerks to complete the deportation quota; otherwise they themselves and their families would be part of the transport. This threat did its work, and already on the same day, fifteen hundred Jews were assembled. On the twelfth of May a train set out from Sosnowiec on which there were fifteen hundred Jews from Sosnowiec on their way to Auschwitz. The Germans allowed Rabbi Englard to get off the train, but he refused to abandon the rest of the Jews in their time of strife and in the end, he was killed together with them. *Pinkas Hakehillot Polin:* "Sosnowiec," Jewish Gen.org.

# CHAPTER 5

# MY HUSBAND AND FELLOW SURVIVOR: HENRY ROSENBLATT

## Meeting Henry: 1941

My parents sent me to my aunt Rushka and uncle Leon's house to get money for medicine for my aunt Franya. We were running out of money because we were supporting and feeding so many people in our home. I went with my girlfriend Hanka Banker, who lived in our building. As we entered my aunt's building, I passed a group of boys standing in the hallway waiting for the trolley. [18]

My aunt Rushka's house was in front of a main trolley stop and there was always a crowd of Jews waiting outside her building. Jews weren't allowed to use the trolley except at specific times. The Jewish police stood guard and made sure that no one got on until the permitted time. Jews often snuck on anyway because it was so packed with people. Even I sometimes snuck on

---

[18] Hanka was with me in Grünberg and survived the war. She became Hanka Appelbaum, and I saw her again in Acre, Israel.

and tried to hide my yellow star with "Jude" written on it. It was risky because if you were caught, you were beaten or possibly deported, and sometimes shot.

It was on this day in April 1941 that I first met my future husband, Henry (Henriek/Chil) Rosenblatt. Henry and the other boys had been released from a labor camp in Germany and were trying to return to their homes. Henry lived in Siewierz, a small town outside of Sosnowiec. All the boys were nervous and trying to keep out of sight from the Jewish police because none of them had papers. They hoped to slip onto the trolley without being noticed; being on the street without legal papers could get you arrested or killed, and they were afraid of being arrested again and shipped back to a labor camp.

Unbelievably, this was the second time Henry had been released from a forced labor camp in Germany. He had been picked up in the first days of the war with many Jewish men in his area. By October 1939, he had been deported to Görlitz and Luckenwalde in Germany. The Nazis paraded them through different cities wearing signs that said, "We are the Jews who wanted the war," while the German people spit on them and threw things. The Nazis released Henry in the beginning of 1940, and he returned to Siewierz. A few months later, the Nazis ordered every family to "volunteer" one person to work for the Reich. Henry "volunteered" to protect his brothers, and in November 1940 he was taken to Auenrode concentration camp, which was part of the Schmelt organization. In Auenrode, Henry chopped down trees in the forest, cleared the ground, and laid railroad tracks for the Autobahn. It was winter, cold and snowy, and he only had wooden clogs. A kind nurse in the camp knew Henry and some of the boys and somehow got the camp commandant to release them. They returned to Poland in April 1941, right after Purim.

As we passed the boys, Hanka and I heard the name "Rosenblatt." Rosenblatt was my last name and Hanka urged me to find out if one of them was a relative. I was reluctant to approach the boys because as a Bais Yaakov girl, I didn't speak to strange boys without first being introduced. Hanka thought I was ridiculous, but I didn't talk to them. I nodded to them when we left and noticed that Henry was wearing a scarf around his face.

I went home and told my mother that there was a group of boys at my aunt's apartment building and one of them was named Rosenblatt. She made sandwiches, even though we didn't have a lot of food, and went to speak with the boys and give them the food. My mother realized that Henry was a cousin and she brought him home. When Henry walked into the house, he saw my reflection in the mirror of a big closet door, and he was so surprised. He told my mother that he had just seen me a few minutes ago in the building by the trolley. He didn't understand that I was the reason that my mother had gone to the building to speak to the boys.

My mother told him, "Don't worry. My daughter knows a lot of people and will make you papers." It wasn't easy to get papers, but I knew people in the Jewish Gemeinde and could arrange it. We couldn't take in all the boys and make them papers, and for many years I felt guilty about them because they were all rearrested.

Henry stayed at our house for three days until his papers were ready. We got friendly, especially because he couldn't go anywhere. He was impressed with my energy and how I managed to take care of things. Our personalities were similar. We both took charge of situations and were fighters for ourselves and others. I liked how respectful he was to my parents, but I was afraid he might be too religious for me because he was a yeshiva boy. He asked for a photograph of me before he left.

## Henry and Mira: 1941–1942

When Henry got home, he showed my picture to his two older unmarried brothers, Srulik and Herschel. They teased Henry and told him he was too young to have a girlfriend and they would be better as my boyfriend. Srulik and Herschel had been forced to serve in the Polish army during the mandatory draft and they had become more worldly and less religious. However, Henry was no longer the young, naïve yeshiva boy from before the war. He was twenty-one years old and had spent the last two years working in various slave labor camps for the Reich.

Henry began to visit me in Sosnowiec and brought me a photograph of himself with a warm, very friendly inscription on the back of the picture: "Ofevuje swoja podobizne kusynce, Mirce Rosenblatt" (I offer an image of my face to my cousin, Mirka Rosenblatt). His brothers also visited me and teased me about my growing friendship with Henry. Sosnowiec and Siewierz were about ten miles apart and you could find ways to travel between the two towns if you had the right permits. Srulik came most often to visit because he had been in the Polish army and had an upgraded permit.

During this time, another German officer who had been friends with my parents when we all lived together at Piłsudska 64 during World War I approached my parents with a proposition. He was being reposted to Berlin from his administrative position in Sosnowiec. He offered to take me with him as his maid and promised my parents that he wouldn't abuse me. My parents decided to agree to his offer and arranged a time for him to take me. He was older, very tall, and heavy with ugly skin. I didn't want to go with him and I didn't want to leave my parents. I refused to go and ran away to Henry's house on Oleśnickiego Street #13, also known as Zaidels Street, in Siewierz.

I stayed with Henry for three days and met his family: his father, stepmother, and sister Sarah. It wasn't proper for me to sleep in the same house with boys so I stayed next door in his married brother Yankel's house. I got close with all of them and when I left, his brothers gave me a photograph with both of them in it, as did his sister Sarah. The pictures had the same sentiment written in Polish, "Sympatyczney," which meant to show their strong warm feelings toward me.

Nobody thought about love because of the times, but we were all of the age where you thought about boys or girls and it was natural to have these kinds of feelings. Henry was very sure about his feelings toward me. I felt unsure and too young to focus on one person. We weren't boyfriend and girlfriend, just good friends. I didn't know what I thought or felt—we liked each other but it was the war and crazy times and who thought about love? Henry continued to visit and we grew closer. I have a picture of Henry dated March 2, 1942, where he wrote in beautiful romantic Polish, "I offer my picture, how I look, to my cousin, Mirce Rosenblatt," which meant, "I give you a piece of me and please remember me."

Henry was able to visit me in Sosnowiec because he had a travel permit from the Nazi officers in Siewierz. His father's small grocery store had been confiscated by the Nazis but Henry and his father continued to manage it. Henry was ordered to restock the store from supplies in Sosnowiec and he came on a regular basis. This is the way he got to know my family. I also got to know his family, even his cousins. Henry had a cousin, Sydney Schlesinger, who looked just like him. They were very close. Sydney's wife got caught in a roundup and was arrested in Będzin and sent to the Dulag in Sosnowiec in 1941. Henry and Sydney came to me and pleaded with me to use my connections with the Jewish Gemeinde to get her released. It was too late—she was already on a train. [19]

Our families became close. Sometimes my family helped Henry find goods for the store so he wouldn't get into trouble. Henry tried to rescue me before I was deported to my labor camp and he tried as much as possible to sneak food into the Srodula ghetto for my siblings once I was deported.

In normal times, Henry and I would have met each other's families. But in these times it was rather unique that we got to do so. It created a special connection between Henry and me. We were lucky that we each had memories of each other's families since most survivors never had that opportunity.

I continued to work in the Held factory and Henry continued his visits and life went on. More of our loved ones, friends, and neighbors were arrested and deported. Life continued to get worse daily and yet Henry and I moved toward a deeper relationship. We never made any formal commitments, but our relationship grew stronger. And then I was gone.

## Henry: 1942–1943

On August 12, 1942, the Great Deportation of Sosnowiec Jews took place. I was "selected" for slave labor at an arbeitslager and shipped to Grünberg. I

[19] Sydney survived the war and remarried. His wife's name was Helen and we remained very close throughout the years. Sydney lived to one hundred years old and had over one hundred descendants when he died in 2020.

heard from other girls who arrived later from Sosnowiec that Henry heard about the Great Aktion and came to the Dulag with money to buy my freedom. Unfortunately, he came one day too late; I was already on the train. However, maybe I was fortunate, because if I had stayed in Sosnowiec, I may not have survived.

I heard occasional news about Henry from new arrivals in the camp. I also heard about Henry from my sisters. At some point, we were allowed to mail letters while I was in Grünberg. I wrote two postcards to my sister Estusha and I received a postcard from Estusha, a postcard from Vida Malka, and a postcard from Henry.

Vida Malka wrote that life was very bad at Targowa 21 and sometimes Henry brought them food. Estusha wrote that she and the children, Natan, Helusha, and Meitush, had been relocated into the Srodula ghetto and were registered under the family name. Food was very scarce but sometimes Henry snuck into the ghetto and brought them something to eat. By 1944, I didn't hear from anyone anymore. I heard from the new girls arriving at Grünberg that many towns were liquidated and Jews were being sent directly to Auschwitz to be gassed to death. Sometime in late 1944, I received a postcard from Henry from Lagischa, a subcamp of Auschwitz, where he wrote simply, "Stay strong and hope."

Henry had a long and horrible war and suffered greatly during the Holocaust. I didn't know what he went through until after the war. When I first met him in the spring of 1941, he had been arrested two separate times by the Nazis and been shipped to slave labor camps where he did hard labor for months. Somehow, Henry was released both times, either through luck or through his own shrewdness. Once I got Henry his papers, he left Sosnowiec and returned to his family in Siewierz on April 10, 1941. In June 1942, the Jews were expelled from Siewierz and resettled into the Zawiercie ghetto. Henry lived in the ghetto with his father, stepmother, sister Sarah, brothers Herschel and Srulik, and Yankel with his wife Hindela and four children. I knew about Henry's resettlement to Zawiercie but I didn't know anything else because I had already been shipped to Grünberg. In Zawiercie, Henry worked at the Luftwaffelanger, a factory/laundry for uniforms for the air force. The Zawiercie ghetto was liquidated between August and October 1943. Henry was deported on October 18, 1943—the last deportation of Jews from Zawiercie. He was shipped directly to Auschwitz and was "selected" to work. His new identity was the number tattooed on his forearm: #157756. Henry worked at Auschwitz's subcamps of Lagischa, Jaworzno, and Golleschau. In January 1945, Auschwitz was abandoned, and he was forced onto the Death March to Blechhammer and Buchenwald concentration camps. Henry was freed from Flossenbürg concentration camp on April 23, 1945.

Henry before the War, 1939

Henry's family, c. 1936. L to R: sister-in-law, Hindela, his brother Yankel's wife; his niece, Esther, Yankel's daughter; his brother, Yankel; his brother, Abraham in the cap; his sister-in-law, Hinda, Abraham's wife in front.

Henry's brother Srulik with the Jewish Star with German photographers, overseeing Polish workers, 1940

Left: Henry's brother Herschel, Siewierz 1938

Right: Henry's cousin Mayer Wajcman, Siewierz 1942 (He was with Henry in the first days of the war. Survived and lived in Israel)

Henry's sister Sarah,
Siewierz 1942

Henry's brothers
Srulik and Herschel,
Siewierz 1942

Henry gave me this picture with loving inscription
dated March 2, 1942

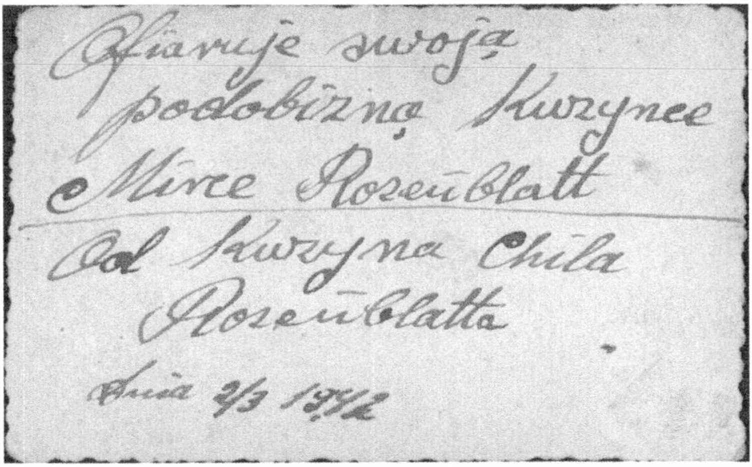

Ofiaruję swoją
podobiznę Kuzynce
Mirce Rosenblatt
Od Kuzyna Chila
Rosenblatta
Sucha 2/3 1942

Henry's inscription on March 2, 1942 picture: "I offer you how I look to my cousin," which was a romantic way of saying, please remember me

## CHAPTER 6

# THE GREAT DEPORTATION: AUGUST 12, 1942

On August 11, 1942, the Nazis ordered all twenty-six thousand Jews of Sosnowiec to report to the sports stadium in the Stary Sosnowiec neighborhood the next day. We had to register for new work permits and have our IDs stamped with a special stamp to get new ration cards. Merin, the head of the Judenrat, notified everyone to be ready early in the morning and not to bring anything with us. This was going to be a routine administrative matter and we were told that we would be home in a few hours. We wouldn't be allowed to work or get food rations without the new stamp, so you had to go.

My parents decided not to take my deceased aunt Franya's two little kids, Helusha and Meitush, with us since they weren't registered and they were so young. We hid them in our coal shed under blankets. They understood the danger and knew to be quiet and stay hidden.

On Wednesday morning, August 12, 1942, the Great Aktion of the Sosnowiec Jews began. It was a beautiful summer day and we dressed in our summer clothes. We were not allowed to take food with us or bring suitcases.

The Gestapo surrounded the ghetto and ordered everyone out of their homes: "All Jews out now." The Jewish police under Merin's Judenrat were responsible for checking each house to make sure everyone was out and then directing us to the stadium. We were thousands of people marching through town in an orderly, calm manner because we thought this was going to secure us with our new papers. Of course, we were afraid because you were always afraid around the SS, but we didn't realize that it was all fake. There was no special stamp, no new rations cards to be issued, and this was not a routine administrative matter. We were marching to selections and deportations to concentration camps or labor camps. Most of us were never coming home again. [20]

I left my home on Targowa Street with my mother and my father, with Vida Malka, Estusha, and Natan wearing sensible shoes and coats over our summer clothes. We joined the throngs of Jews marching to the stadium. We didn't pack a suitcase because we were just going to get new papers, not to be "resettled."

The Jewish police kept all of us walking straight to the stadium on Mireckiego Aleja with no detours while the SS watched from the sides. People walked quietly with their families and I don't remember anyone resisting. It took about an hour to walk to the stadium because there were so many people.

The SS and Gestapo took charge once we entered the stadium and all the calmness ended abruptly. There were so many people already there by the time we got there, and it was terribly noisy and chaotic. People were frantically looking for other family members. The Gestapo made their "selections" as we entered and separated us into groups. I was "selected" to join a group of teenage girls and my family was pushed forward. I lost sight

---

[20] The Nazis deliberately misled the Jews into thinking this was not a deportation by telling them not to bring suitcases. They wanted this large Aktion to go smoothly and have less hysteria among the people, so they lied to make it seem like a bureaucratic action rather than the Great Aktion. Natan Eliasz Szternfinkel, "Destruction of the Jewish Population of Sosnowiec" (Kattowitz, Poland, 1946 in Polish, unpublished), Jewishgen.org/yizkor/Sosnowiec/Sosnowiec.html. Translated privately by the Robinson Family in memory of Amalie Mary Reichman Robinson in 2000. Anne Marie Reichman Robinson was #47746 at Grünberg of KL Gross Rosen; Mira Rosenblatt was #47313.

of them and had no idea if they were together or what had happened. I was all alone. I kept looking for them but couldn't see any of them. I pleaded with the SS guard watching my group to let me go and find my family.

I stood in that stadium all day long, in the hot sun with no food and no idea of what was happening while more and more Jews kept coming. In the evening, it began to rain hard and the grounds became very muddy. The SS guards began to ride their horses through the crowd, making more mud and beating everyone they passed with their truncheons. People fell down into the mud and were screaming, "Where is G-d; where is my G-d?" It was very frightening. No one knew what was happening, but it was clear that we were not going back home anytime soon.

I continued to plead with the guard to let me try to find my family. Finally when it was dark, he allowed me to go. He told me "to get lost" but warned me to return because he would get into trouble if his count was off because of my absence.

I searched the crowds in the dark, muddy, packed stadium for my family, screaming out their names. It took more than an hour before I spotted them huddled all together in a group that did not look like it would be considered for a work detail.

I was so happy to see them but so afraid for them. Their group wasn't going to a labor camp—they were either too young or too old. My father looked old with his torn face from his ripped-out beard from the first days of the war, my beautiful and young-looking mother also looked older standing next to him, Estusha and Natan looked like the little kids they were, and Vida Malka looked too delicate.

My mother and I tried to think of a plan to stay together but we couldn't. I told my mom, "Vida Malka should come with me as well as Esther and Natan and then maybe you can sneak into another line and save yourself. You are young-looking and beautiful." My mother answered, "How can I get away from here—I don't even know where we're going or when and I am not going to leave your father." I asked her if I should stay with them. In the end we decided it would be better if I took my siblings and returned to my group. Maybe we would all have a chance then.

I kissed my parents and told them that I loved them and to stay strong. They told me they loved me and that I should stay strong and take care of my sisters and brother. I didn't know that this was the last time I would see my parents.

I hurried back to my group with my siblings because of my promise to the SS guard. He didn't say anything about my siblings joining the group; maybe he didn't even notice them with all the people around. Sometime early in the morning, the Gestapo marched my whole group of about one hundred to two hundred girls, with Vida Malka, Estusha, Natan, and myself, out of the stadium toward the Dulag.

We were in my old neighborhood in Stary Sosnowiec. I was marching through the streets where I had grown up. I knew every house and yard that we passed; I knew many of the people who still lived there. They were our Polish neighbors who had shopped in our store and watched me grow up. I even knew the stadium where we had been held for the past two days because it was the same stadium that I used to sneak into to watch sporting events before the war.

We walked out of the stadium and passed the old Kornfeld's bookstore and then the horse smith where I used to climb over the fence from my backyard to play. We passed my old house on Piłsudska Street and turned the corner onto Stara Street and continued to Składowa Street to the Dulag. Along the way we passed a private house with a large garden behind a fence that had two broken boards. I looked at Estusha and Natan and knew that they couldn't pass as sixteen-year-olds and would never be selected to work in a labor camp. They were just little kids, nine and twelve years old. I made an impulsive decision that I had to get them off the line of marchers. As we passed the large garden by the private house, I quickly pushed them and Vida Malka through the broken boards into the garden.

The Gestapo marched alongside to make sure no one escaped but there were so many people marching, it was hard to control everything. I planned to wait a minute or two and then sneak off the line also. I had this crazy idea that when things calmed down, I could go to our old neighbors and maybe someone would help us. We were marching right past their houses, and they knew me and they knew my family. I hoped for kindness.

I never had the chance to sneak off the line. One of the Jewish girls in my group called out to the SS guard and pointed to me and said, "Look, look at her, she is trying to run away." He put his rifle on my shoulder and marched me into the Dulag—he never left my side for a minute.

I was desperate, more desperate than I ever was in my life, before or after. Vida Malka, Estusha, and Natan were in the garden because of my actions. They were all alone and had no plan or any idea of what to do next. And I couldn't help them, even though I had promised my parents I would take care of them.

There hasn't been a day that has passed since August 13, 1942, that I haven't thought back to that fateful moment when I pushed the three of them into the garden. I have been filled with guilt and have never been able to come to terms with it. I felt personally responsible for their deaths all my life. My impulsive act of trying to save them only guaranteed their deaths. My sister Vida Malka was old enough and strong enough to be sent to a labor camp with me. Who was I to have made the decision to push her into the garden with the kids? The brutal irony was that the SS guard who put his gun on my shoulder was my savior. If I had snuck off the line to go to my sisters and brother, I would have been sent to Auschwitz with them. The labor camp was my chance to survive.

I was in the Dulag for two days before our group of girls was deported to Grünberg, a labor camp that was part of the Gross-Rosen concentration camp network.

The Aktion of August 12, 1942, forced twenty-six thousand Jews into the Umschlagplatz. A small group was allowed to go home as they were considered to be essential workers for the war effort, and a large group was selected to be sent to forced labor camps. Between eight and ten thousand Jews were selected to be deported to Auschwitz to be gassed. My mother and father were two of those selected to be gassed to death. I wanted to know if my parents were shipped out immediately or languished for days in the upstairs rooms of the Dulag because the Nazis didn't have enough trains. It was important for me to know if their end was quick or tortured. As much as I tried, I never learned the details of their last days.

Vida Malka, Estusha, and Natan survived the deportation of August 1942 but did not survive the war. I don't know how they made it to walk two miles home to Targowa 21. They had to cross big streets and it was so far. They were so young, maybe somebody helped them. They did make it home and rescued the little ones out of the coal shed. They stayed together in the apartment, managing to get food to feed everyone and trying to stay out of sight because of how young they all were. I learned later that Vida Malka was taken in an Aktion in late 1942 and deported to Neusalz labor camp. Neusalz was considered a decent work camp and many girls survived, but unfortunately Vida Malka did not. I believe that she died in the first days of the Death March.

My twelve-year-old sister, Estusha, was responsible for my little brother, Natan, who was ten years old, Helusha, who was four years old, and Meitush, who was two years old. Early in 1943, the entire Sosnowiec ghetto was liquidated, and the Jews were resettled into the Srodula ghetto. Estusha registered under another name and was able to get a room for them. Life was miserable for everyone in Srodula and even more so for my sister and brother because they were so young and had to manage all by themselves. My aunt Rushka and her family were there as well, and I hoped they helped them as much as possible. Henry also tried to help them when he could. Srodula was liquidated before the end of 1943 and my beautiful, wonderful sister, brother, and cousins were sent to the gas chambers of Auschwitz. [21]

---

[21] http://www.holocaustresearchproject.org/nazioccupation/sosbend.html. See also Edward Gastfriend, *My Father's Testament: Memoir of a Jewish Teenager, 1938–1945* (Philadelphia: Temple University Press, 2000), pp. 55–71.

Deportation of the Jews from the Sosnowiec Ghetto

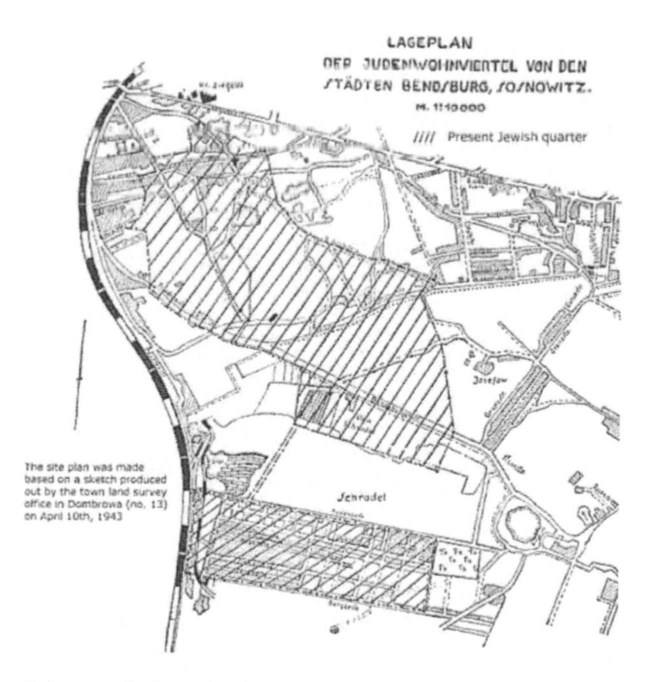


Map outlining the Sosnowiec and Srodula Ghettos

Dienst Stadium
PILSUDSKIEGO
64 Pilsudskiego
Dulag
SKLADOWA
STARA
MATKI
PILSUDSKIEGO

21 Targowa
3 MAJA
MODRZEJOWSKA
TARGOWA

# CHAPTER 7

# GRÜNBERG CONCENTRATION CAMP: AUGUST 1942–JANUARY 1945

## First Days at Grünberg

The Nazis marched my group of girls from the stadium through my old neighborhood to the Dulag. We were quickly processed, and the next day we were put on regular train cars and deported for work detail to Grünberg concentration camp in Zielona Góra. I looked out the window and watched my old world, once filled with sweet memories and now shattered by the horrors of the last few days, fade away into the distance. It has remained unbelievable and incomprehensible to me for all these years that my final times with my family were back in my old neighborhood—that the last tortuous moments of my family should have taken place in the area where we had shared all the best moments of our lives.

It took us less than a day to get to Grünberg, which was on the border between Poland and Germany, about one and a half hours from Berlin. We were to become the slave laborers who replaced the German workers at

DeutscherWoollenManufactur (DWM) at 33 Wrocławska Strasse. Lalush Neukirchner, brother-in-law of the notorious Nazi leader Hermann Göring, was in charge of the factory. It was a large, modern factory that employed more than fifteen hundred workers and had previously been owned by a British company.

I arrived in Grünberg as a passenger in a regular railroad car train, not a cattle car like others, and almost believed that I was being "resettled" to become a valued worker in the German war machine. I thought perhaps it would be like life in the ghetto. I quickly realized that life in Grünberg was very different. Grünberg was an evil, horrible place and was known to be a terrible labor camp because there were so many cruel, vicious people in charge. [22]

Upon arrival, the female SS guards lined us up and made us undress. Then they shaved or cut our hair and powdered us with disinfection. We had to stand naked in a circle while the male SS guards inspected us for work selection. I thought I would die of shame. I thought this was the worst thing that could happen to me; little did I know what the next three years of my life were going to be like. I passed the examination and was given a ragged uniform with a number on it; that number patched in the front and the back became my identity. I was no longer Mira and my earlier life was erased. I was #47313.

## Life in Grünberg

Our barrack was a large building across the street from the factory. There were a thousand to fifteen hundred girls sleeping there. We slept three girls in one bed with three bunks stacked on top of one another, and in one corner

---

[22] The conditions at Grünberg were atrocious according to Gerda Klein and others (Klein, *All But My Life* [New York: Hill and Wang, 1957], p. 168). The US Holocaust Museum described the conditions at Grünberg, stating, "Conditions worsened. Although officially approved by the Gross-Rosen provisions department, the food was almost a starvation diet." "The Spinnerei," *Journey Through The Holocaust*, accessed July 14, 2020, https://journeythroughtheholocaust.org/items/show/18, p. 742. Along with the food situation or lack thereof, the prisoners would be beaten for any slight discretion by the guards. Klein, *All But My Life*, chapters 10, 11, and 12.

there were a few sinks. We had a small blanket and a pillow, but I don't remember if there were mattresses, maybe some straw. The roof had skylights and sometimes I could see the moon or stars but never the sun. There were nights when I looked up and could see it snowing; it looked so beautiful and pure. In front of the barrack was a courtyard with a big tree known as the "Hanging Tree," which the SS guards used to punish us.

Our wake-up time was 4:30 a.m. and we rushed to wash up and eat our meager breakfast. You had to keep yourself clean; otherwise you had no chance to survive. The Germans called us "Dirty Jews, you smell" and told us, "You can use the soap because it's made from your parents' bones." Breakfast was some ersatz coffee and a hard piece of bread, sometimes with a little piece of margarine. By 5:00 a.m., we lined up for the Appell, which was a miserable part of our day. It was roll call—twice a day we stood in lines and the SS guards counted us over and over again. On a regular day, the Appell would take at least an hour and then there were so many days and nights when we stood for hours and hours because of one issue or another. On Sundays, the Appell always lasted two to three hours. It was really difficult to stand straight and not move. If you moved or swayed the guards kicked you or pulled you out of the line and beat you up. I was never sure whether it was worse to stand in the freezing cold or in the hot sun. We did this twice a day, every day, for the three years I was there. Once the Appell was approved, the women guards marched us to the factory.

We got very little food, and if we didn't work hard enough we were punished and received no food at all. Everything we ate was made with spinach and dirt. At night we got soup with dirt in it and another piece of bread made with potato and flour.

There were 100 to 150 men in our camp at different times and they worked in the fields. They finished work earlier than the girls in the factory and got better food. The girls working in the kitchen wanted to get in good with the men, so they gave them thicker soups, sometimes with a potato and even stronger coffee.

The kitchen girls were the luckiest in the camp because they were able to get more food and the work wasn't that hard. I don't know how these girls were chosen, but they were the most fortunate. Some of the girls tried to help the rest of us and some were cruel. The girls who worked in the "Risserei" sometimes found diamonds and traded them for food. I got lucky once because one of the men who worked in the orchard, Wasserman, snuck me four rotten apples. One of the girls—Sarah—had been a maid in my uncle Shimon Baer's house and was uncomfortable around me. She was friendly with Favel Panski, who was related to Henry, and gave him extra food when she could. They fell in love, but she died on the Death March. [23]

Another person who worked in the kitchen was Mrs. Kornfeld/Zambrani, who came to Grünberg a few months after me. I remember how shocked I was to see her. She never gave me any extra food or helped me. Once she reported me when I took a sliver of carrot from the kitchen floor, and I got slapped twice across the face by the Judenelteste, the female Jewish supervisor.

Every day we marched back to our barracks in rows for two blocks and passed a theater and a garden. The garden had grapes and other fruits and we dreamed of tasting those fruits. The best we could do was sneak some grass to chew. We had to walk in straight lines on the street or we were beaten with a steel pipe with a rubber handle. Many times, people were standing outside all dressed, ready to go to the theater. These German people saw us, exhausted and starving and half dead, and never said anything to us. After the war, they acted like they didn't know anything about what was going on right under their noses.

We left the factory at 6:00 p.m. and lined up for another Appell in the courtyard in front of our barracks. Sometimes they put us to work unloading potatoes and cabbage before we got anything to eat. If the guards thought you weren't working hard enough, they beat you on the back or on your legs with the steel pipe as punishment.

I didn't know what happened to my family.

---

[23] I helped Favel Panski after the war when he was in the hospital with tuberculosis. He apologized for not sharing his extra food with me. Favel emigrated to Israel and I visited him often. Our families are still in touch.

## Working in the Factory

We worked twelve-hour shifts starting at 6:00 a.m. There were day and night shifts, and in the beginning, I worked the day shift. We were manufacturing material and making uniforms, blankets, etc., for the German military. It was hard, difficult work.

I learned all about manufacturing fabric and the processes needed from working at the factory. You started by ripping up the old cloth, "Risserei"; making the thread, "Kramperlei"; spinning the thread, "Spinnerei"; putting the thread on spools, "Spoolerei"; and weaving, "Vaberei."

Every day, boxes filled with old clothes arrived from Auschwitz. The first part of the process was to unpack and sort the material. The girls assigned to this job sometimes found valuables, even diamonds and gold. They sewed the valuables into their clothes or swallowed them. One girl knitted skirts and hid the diamonds that way. Everyone was afraid that they might recognize a piece of clothing that once belonged to a family member. The material then went to the Risserei, where the old clothes were ripped up. The next step in the process was the Kramperlei.

I was assigned to the Kramperlei and was responsible for three big, heavy machines that used to be operated by men. Each machine was the size of a dining room and I had to run from one machine to the next to keep the process going. I threw the ripped sorted clothes mixed with wool and a pressed wood called "torf" into one machine and a beige, cottony-type fabric came out of my second machine on big rollers. Then the heavy cotton rollers went into my third machine with a metal stick. The threads had to be even so they wouldn't rip, but the material itself was of poor quality and it ripped often.

My first machine was connected to my second machine with a wooden ladder that made eight-foot rolls of cotton that were rolled onto larger rollers of fabric. These rollers were made of heavy stainless-steel rods covered with wood, with a three-inch stainless-steel handle on each end. The handles helped us lift these large rolls and transfer them to the third machine. A bell would ring, and I had to move two of these incredibly heavy rolls using the handles and all the strength in my legs, arms, and body to position them in the right place. You had to be careful not to rip the fabric because it was soft. I had to do this all alone. The third machine made threads from the cotton, which were wound around four wooden sticks, each about twenty-four inches long. The sticks were horizontally connected to a metal frame at the corners. I had to watch the threads as they wound around the sticks to make sure they didn't rip. One of my jobs was to take sample threads and weigh them to see if the wool was the correct weight for the fabrics. This was really the foreman's job, but I learned to do it myself.

The machines broke down often and if the threads ripped, the guards would beat you and if you didn't meet your quota, you were punished with three hours of extra work. I learned how to adjust the machines to make them run right and could fix my machines myself. The technicians couldn't believe that this little dirty Jewish girl could be so handy. One of the foremen hated me even more because I could help myself. I was lucky that the head technician liked me because I worked well and kept the machines going.

The next process was the Spinnerei, where the frame with the full sticks of thread was taken to be spun onto spools. The foreman of the Spinnerei was very mean and rough on the girls. He had a pointy chin and we nicknamed him Gembelo (German for "chin"). Gembelo slapped and beat us in passing and we were scared to be near him. One time, as I was helping fix another girl's machine, the threads on my machine got tangled and Gembelo took the entire frame of wood and threads and threw it at me. I ducked and the frame hit the window behind me and broke it. He got nervous about the broken window, so he left me alone. [24]

---

[24] In the late spring of 1945, I was walking by the railroad tracks in Streidelsdorf where I was pretending to be a Polish girl. A Polish soldier started to flirt with me and as we walked along, I saw Gembelo hiding in the ticket booth waiting to sneak onto the train. I told the Polish soldier that I had worked in a factory under Gembelo and told him how mean and cruel he was. The Polish soldier wanted me to shoot him myself with his gun. I refused and we brought a shaking Gembelo to the Polish army to be arrested. Unbelievably, twenty years later, in 1965, I was in Hot Springs, Arkansas, for mineral bath treatments when this "Polish soldier" walked into my hotel. He wasn't a former Polish soldier—he was a fellow Jewish survivor named Mike Suhl. I hadn't seen Mike since that day in 1945 and never knew he was Jewish! Mike remained a flirt and I told my husband he'd better join me soon. Henry came the next day! The three of us became friends and saw one another often because Mike lived in New Jersey.

One day, my dress got caught in the third machine and I had to tear it off so I wouldn't get pulled into the machine. My dress getting stuck caused the machine to stop. There I was, wearing only my panties in front of a stopped machine. The head technician threw me his own work coat to cover myself, which was an unusual act of kindness and not permitted. He had pity on me because I was a good worker and he didn't want to lose me. He was a kind man—sometimes he threw his leftover food in the garbage for me to get later to eat. He stopped when his wife complained that he was losing weight.

During this incident, I got a deep cut on my forearm that became infected. There was a red stripe running down my arm that kept growing as the infection got worse. I was in terrible pain and couldn't really use my hand anymore. I tried to keep working my three machines with my head, my leg, and any other way I could. The foreman saw how much pain I was in and, as a good deed, he sent me to the infirmary for medical attention. The nurse sat me down next to a table with sharp instruments and told me she was going to cut off my right hand. If she cut off my hand, I was as good as dead. When the nurse turned away, I quickly took two of the instruments and stabbed myself as hard as I could into the infection. The pus spurted out all over the place. The nurse ran over, hit me across the face, called me "Dirty Jew," and continued to beat me while I lay on the floor. Later she bandaged me up; I kept screaming, "My hand, my hand," because it was numb and I was afraid maybe the nurse had amputated my hand. After ten days, I healed and took the bandage off.

We had to stop to clean out the machines very often, sometimes twice a day. The thread was poor quality and ripped easily and the machines shut down. We lay on our stomachs and used a T-shaped piece of wood with a rod about ten feet long to clean out the threads and dirt stuck in the machine. We had to be careful that the wood T-stick wouldn't get caught in the machine while we were doing this.

Once, I was lying on the floor cleaning the machine and one of the technicians restarted the machine on purpose. My wooden T-stick got caught in the mechanics and the entire machine exploded! All the metal pieces of the Krempererai went flying and the damage was extensive. There was a whole commotion, and everyone came running.

I was accused of sabotage and the head foreman, Lalush Neukirchner, was called to the factory to handle the situation. I thought this would be the end for me. Lalush was mean and everyone was afraid of him. He wore a big ring and hit the girls in the face with it. If you were lucky, you only got a black eye, but sometimes the ring ripped the girl's face apart.

They dragged me out from under the machine but left me on the floor. I couldn't stand up because I was shaking like a fish. They called me "farfluchted Yudde"—"dirty Jew"—and a saboteur. I was afraid they would shoot me on the spot. The head technician who liked my work stood up for me and told Lalush that I was one of the best workers, reliable, and that I could fix all the machines.

Again, I was lucky, and I was only punished, not beaten or sent to Auschwitz. My punishment was that I was responsible for six machines instead of three for the next three months and I now worked on the first floor instead of the second floor. Hanka Keller, a German Jewish girl, helped me so much during this time, along with some of the other girls, because it was almost impossible to manage six of these large machines.

## Life in Grünberg Continues

At one point, we were allowed to write letters. I wrote two postcards home and told my sister Estusha to lie about her age and try to come to Grünberg. Estusha wrote back and told me they got home from the garden and rescued Helusha and Meitus from the shed. She wrote that she couldn't come because she had to be a mother to the little children. Amazingly, she sent me a package of clothing with a beautiful blue shirt and shoes.

I never got to wear any of the clothing Estusha sent me because the Judenelteste—our female Jewish supervisor—took the package away from me. When I told her it was my package, she hit me in the face. She wore the clothes and taunted me.

The Judenelteste's name was Eva Messer and she was vicious and cruel. Everyone hated her. She was blond and beautiful and came from Sosnowiec where she was involved with criminals. As a Judenelteste, Eva had power and control over us even though she was Jewish. There was another Judenelteste, Minna Singer, who was much nicer and tried to help us. The Judeneltestes reported to female kapos, who reported to the SS men.

Eva Messer, the mean Judenelteste, punished me and made me work extra hours because she accused me of working too slowly. It was obviously a lie because I never worked slowly on anything. During this time when I was working the extra hours, a Hungarian girl was cooking two stolen potatoes on the steam pipe in the factory. Her shift was finished but the potatoes were still raw. She offered me one of them if I brought her the other potato when I finished my shift. Of course I said yes, but I was unlucky this time and got caught with the potatoes by the guards. Eva Messer made me stand outside in the freezing cold—standing "straight" for three hours. I wasn't allowed to bend my knees and when my knees buckled, she kicked me in the back of my knees and yelled, "Stand up straight." I almost fainted during the punishment and could barely walk to my bunk at the end. Two girls came out and dragged me inside. They gave me some water to revive me and tried to warm me up.

I shared my bunk with Chana Pinkus from Będzin. She was a deeply religious girl and had been a Bais Yaakov teacher. We became close friends and supported each other, but she didn't share with me how horrible her situation was. I knew she worked extra hours, sometimes sixteen hours a day, and was struggling to survive. Sometimes, I felt her body burning up next to mine as we lay in the bunk. She worked the night shift in the Spinnerei department and the foreman in that department was known to be a terrible man who molested the girls. I didn't realize what was going on and that the foreman was satisfying himself with her and beating her at the same time. One day, Chana couldn't get up to go to work and our Judenelteste, Eva Messer, told the female kapos, who came to check on her. They pulled the blanket off her and her body was all cut up—her breasts, her stomach, her private area. The kapos asked her how this happened; she told them that the foreman had done this to her. The kapos then beat her up for accusing a good German man with her lies. She was crying terribly and I wanted to stay with her, but they forced me to report to my work shift. When I came back,

Chana Pinkus was gone and I never saw her again. I wished we had hidden her in her bed and maybe she would have been able to heal and survive. The other girls told me that Chana had scribbled a note to me on some of her pictures but some of the other girls ripped them up.

There was one girl that ran away from the camp and didn't get caught. She planned her escape with one of the German girls who worked in the factory who arranged a hiding place for her. After the kapos realized that one of us was missing during the Appell, they threatened to hang ten of us. We stood for hours as they deliberated on what to do, but in the end, no one was hanged.

If you were sick or hurt and couldn't work, you were no good and were killed. There was an infirmary and one of the doctors tried to help. He covered up for people who couldn't walk and gave them time to recuperate in the infirmary without telling the SS. In 1943 or 1944, a group of SS doctors came to Grünberg to make sure no one had tuberculosis. The doctors sat at a long table and we stood naked in front of them as they examined us and then had us get x-rayed. Anyone with tuberculosis was sent immediately to Auschwitz.

Sometime in 1944, a surprising event happened when a group of weakened, sick girls were sent to Denmark in exchange for oil that didn't freeze. I was good friends with two of the girls who were included in the exchange. Both had been injured working with the big machines in the factory; one was the sister of my friend Karol Tuchschneider, who had a bad limp after injuring her leg, and the other girl, Schievik, was a short little girl whose hand had to be amputated. We used to share our soup and spoon it directly into her mouth to keep her alive. Schievik survived and ultimately ended up in Chicago. Karol's sister died from pneumonia in Denmark and was buried there. Many years later, I met Karol in Israel and told him what happened with his sister and he arranged to move her remains to Israel.

Survival meant helping each other. I tried whenever I could to help the other girls, especially by fixing their machines. There were so many times when different girls helped me as well. You had to help each other; otherwise there was no way you could make it. In the camps, every day you had no choice but to go on. I thought and hoped that after the war, I would see my family, and that kept me going. Life went on day by day.

New transports of girls arrived from the Aktions taking place throughout occupied Europe as the Nazis liquidated the ghettos one by one. This was how we learned some news about the outside world. I didn't know what happened to my family, but I began to hear more news. I heard that all the Jews in the stadium during the Aktion of August 1942 were deported to Auschwitz or labor camps. I heard that the remaining Jews of Sosnowiec were forced to move into the Srodula ghetto in 1943. I learned that Estusha registered under another name, possibly my parents' name, to get a room in Srodula. [25]

After the war, I learned what a horrible, horrible place Srodula was—there was no work, no food, no organization, just a nearby train depot waiting to deport the next group of Jews to Auschwitz. The ghetto was liquidated by the end of 1943 and most of the Jews were sent directly to Auschwitz. Some were sent to the Warsaw ghetto to clean up after the uprising, like Sydney Schlesinger, my husband's cousin.

In mid-1944, girls arrived from other labor camps that were being abandoned because of the Russian advance. In September, the Hungarian Jewish girls began to arrive. They were much stronger than we were and were able to work faster and harder. They looked so much healthier and that made it difficult for us Polish Jewish girls. We had been at Grünberg for three years, doing hard labor, on a starvation diet and being beaten regularly. Some of the Hungarian girls said, "We're strong and you're skinny and dying. Give us your food so we can live." Some of them beat us. And some were nice, like the girl who tried to share her two potatoes with me.

The Russians were fighting close by and sometimes the factory was hit by falling shrapnel and we had to put out fires. In the last days of the war, Grünberg got a new director who was nice and tried to be kinder to us. He tried to get us gas masks because of the bombings. When the orders came to

---

[25] "#152 Rozenblat Szalja Szlama I. date of birth: 22.5.1882," "Verzeichnie No. 54 der Juden, welche aus dem Bereucg des II. Pol. Rev. nach dem III. Pol. Rev./ Schrodel/uberisedelt wurden, p.26. List No. 54, #152.

evacuate Grünberg, he wanted to leave us in the camp to wait for the oncoming Russian army. The decision, however, was that we had to join the Death March.

## Grünberg Is Evacuated

In January 1945, there were about 1,500 girls and about 150 men in Grünberg. We heard the sounds of artillery day and night and knew that the Russians were advancing against the German army. It seemed like the war might be drawing to an end but we didn't know how much we still had to suffer before we would be free. We were counting the days and forcing ourselves to hold on for one day, and then for another day. No one wanted to die when the end was so close, but we were so weak.

In mid-January, a large group of girls arrived at Grünberg after their camps were evacuated. They had been marching in the bitter cold for over a week and they looked terrible. On January 29, 1945, the Nazis lined us all up for our final Appell at Grünberg and we joined the Death March along with thousands of others.

We didn't know that Auschwitz had been liberated two days earlier, on January 27. On February 14, 1945, the Russians liberated Grünberg and continued their advance to Germany. The war was rapidly ending, but not for us. [26]

---

[26] The 2007 revised version of the text on the commemorative plaque at Gruenberg read as follows: "Here in the former wool factory Deutsche Wollenwaren Manufaktur AG about 1,000 Jewish women and 180 Jews men were made to do forced work. . . . [I]t was a branch of the concentration camp in Groß-Rosen. On the 29th of January, 1945 one of the longest marches of death of World War II started here. Several hundred of women did not survive this march." This replaced the 1999 plaque, which read, "to commemorate Polish women from the outside camp KZ Groß-Rosen, the ones who were murdered by the Nazis in the years 1944–1945." https://sztetl.org.pl/en/towns/z/141-zielona-gora/116-sites-of-martyrdom/53189-work-camp.

# CHAPTER 8

# 1945

## The Year of Transition: 1945

Nineteen forty-five was the year that I became a "survivor" and got married. The experiences that I endured from January 1945 to January 1946 were astounding. The year was filled with so much upheaval and so many changes that I can't believe that I actually lived through it: concentration camp; death march; escape; hiding as a German girl; on the run; hiding as a Polish girl; protecting myself from the Russian soldiers; rescue by Henry, my future husband; realizing that the members of my family were all dead. My former life was completely destroyed and I moved forward to marriage, freedom, and safety, fleeing to another country to begin a new life.

The challenge to survive when the end of the war was near was probably the most dangerous time because it was total chaos. The Nazis were willing to fight to the last man to save their Third Reich and I was right next to the German border. The fighting was fierce. During that year, I learned that people are people—some are good and some are bad, and it isn't based on nationality or religion. There were Jews, Poles, Germans, and Russians who helped me survive even with a threat to their own lives; and there were Jews, Poles, Germans, and Russians who caused me harm and great pain.

I began the year as an "Untermensch" in Grünberg labor camp, part of the Gross-Rosen concentration camp network in Poland, and ended the year as a free married woman, a survivor, living in Germany. I survived but learned that most of my loved ones were gone, as was the world I had lived in. And yet my almost-boyfriend from the war years, Henry Rosenblatt, survived as well and came to rescue me so we could begin a new life together.

## The Death March: 1945

It was January 1945 and the war—my war—had gone on for five endless years, but I was still alive. I weighed sixty-eight pounds and had a shaved head, and I knew the end was near. We could hear the fighting in the near distance, and the Russians moved closer daily. We felt and saw the growing German anxiety—they didn't know what to do with us as they prepared to evacuate before the Russians reached our area. Some SS men wanted to leave us in the camp alive, some wanted to gas us immediately, and some wanted to take us into Germany so we could continue to work for the war effort. The Umperfehren (headmaster) decided to evacuate the camp and they could always kill us later. Maybe he received orders from above for the decision since all of the concentration camps emptied their barracks and forced us Jews onto the Death March.

Around this time, I was put on an extra work detail sorting clothes after my regular twelve-hour shift. It was difficult to work all day and all night, but it turned out to be lucky for me. Before we evacuated the camp, I swapped my wooden clogs for a pair of men's shoes and put on an extra layer of clothes that I hid under my coat. This made a huge difference on the Death March.

It was brutally cold and snowy—later I learned that it was one of the coldest winters ever. On January 29, 1945, we left Grünberg in two groups of about eight hundred each and joined the Death March, even though, two days earlier, Auschwitz had been liberated by the Russian Army. We marched for about ten days—day and night without stopping, in snow that was up to our knees. Many girls died from blisters on their feet and from the extreme cold and, of course, from hunger. We marched through the forest but not through towns. We stopped at another concentration camp but they wouldn't let us stay and rest there. We ate snow or grass, and if we were lucky, worms or snakes, if we could find any. We walked closer to Germany, away from the Russians. We walked west to Görlitz on the German border, not toward Czechoslovakia like many other groups of Jews. The front was close—only about forty miles away.

We stopped by a ravine so one of the SS guards could go to the bathroom. The guard went far into the forest to do his business. Another girl, named Basha, and I slowly walked away from the group, pretending to have to go to the bathroom. However, we kept walking farther into the forest. There was an overturned tree stump and we laid down and hid in the hole. A group of five girls followed us but the guards saw them. The SS ran after them and shot them dead. I knew two of the girls, Bronia Landau and Jegeska. Jegeska begged the guard to let her live. She cried out to him, "My husband is alive. I just heard the news. We will give you everything. Please let me live." He shot Jegeska in the mouth. Some of the girls from the Death March left the line and stripped the clothes and shoes from the dead girls.

Basha and I were hidden from the road because of the slant of the ravine, but we saw the dead girls from where we were hiding. The line of Jews on the Death March continued marching past the dead girls but no one stopped for a rest or to go to the bathroom because of all the bodies lying on the ground. These girls helped protect us from being discovered and we stayed in our hiding place through the night. That night was long and cold and Basha and I huddled together under the tree stump. We made it through that long night and in the morning, we started on our way.

## I Am a German Girl: 1945

We were near Kalisz in Poland and saw Polish peasants running away from the front lines. They shared their food with us and afterward Basha and I hid under the hay in the upper area of a broken-down barn. In the morning, German soldiers came into the barn and started poking the hay with their bayonets looking for Jews. They found us and took us to the police. We were separated and I could hear Basha screaming as they beat her. I wasn't beaten because I spoke to them in my perfect German and told them I was a German girl from Breslau who had been separated from my parents who had my papers.

They had captured three other girls and they were questioning them as well. They were Jews who had been in Grünberg with us. We recognized each other but didn't let on that we knew each other. I was lucky because I could hold on to my story.

The police gave a soldier the job of turning our group of five girls over to the SS. It was Basha, myself, and the three other girls who had been at Grünberg—two young girls and a thirty-two-year-old woman. I pleaded with the German soldier as we walked. I told him that the war was over and he should do one good thing and that we were young girls who just wanted to live. He told us that he had killed so many people already and maybe it was time to stop. He offered us a sip of coffee and zweibach (hardtack), but I made him taste it first to make sure he wasn't trying to poison us. In the end, he let us go. He told us to run toward the fighting and maybe we would be saved by the Russians. I think he might have killed himself because as we walked on, I heard one shot in the forest.

We saw a small house with a tall chimney in the distance and walked toward it to see if we could get help. This was in Sommerfeld, Germany, which is now Lubsko, Poland. I continued to pretend to be a German girl and spoke only German. There was an old German couple who lived there with a Polish helper. It was a mill where they milled the wheat into flour. They didn't seem to know anything about the war. The house was warm and cozy and the old lady was so nice. She hugged me and welcomed me to stay with them in a bed in their house. I told her I would stay in the barn and do chores. I fed the pigs and horses and peeled and cooked about a hundred pounds of potatoes. The other four girls hid in the barn and I would sneak soup to them. I had to climb up a rickety ladder carefully so the precious soup wouldn't spill. The old lady would say, "Marisha"—that is what she called me—"you are eating a lot of soup but you are so skinny."

There was a German woman and her child living in the next house. She was from Posen and was also on the run. This woman was suspicious of me and threatened to bring the German police to question me. I knew I had to leave quickly, and I told the old woman that I had to go look for my parents and she cried and called me "mein kinde"—"my child"—and told me that she loved me. She gave me a big loaf of bread and some smoked meat, which I divided up among the five of us girls. We were with her for about four weeks. If the Russians weren't in that area raping girls, I would have gone back there because she was an angel to me. I have often thought about this wonderful woman and wished I had gone back to thank her. She was the first person to show me true kindness and love after so many years of brutality and cruelty.

We left the farm and then the older woman in my group betrayed Basha and me. She had arranged an escape plan for her and the other two girls with one of the Polish workers. For four weeks I had worked day and night, feeding the animals, peeling potatoes, then sneaking food to the girls, and after this, the three of them were abandoning Basha and me to the forest. I cried bitter tears and begged her not to leave us. She refused and the three of them left us, cold and alone in the forest. I never got over this betrayal. I can still feel my panic and pain when the girls left us. I don't understand why it hurt so much. I certainly had suffered greater pain throughout the war, but I never was able to come to terms with the feelings of this moment.

Basha and I walked through the forest hearing the fighting in the distance. We found an abandoned hunting hut and stayed there for the night. That night was terrible. It was unbelievably cold, but what I remember most were the sounds of the wild animals. They were so loud and scary and we heard them all night. There was an old rusty hunting rifle in the hut, and I said to

Basha, "Take the gun and shoot me and then shoot yourself." Basha refused and said, "If I shoot you, and can't shoot myself, then I will be left all alone." Morning finally came and we started to walk through the forest.

## I Am a Polish Girl: 1945

We met a Polish man with a cart and asked for his help. I now pretended to be a Polish girl and spoke only Polish. He was afraid to help but he was nice. He had us lie down in his filthy cart and piled old blankets and bags of animal feed over us. He told us he was taking the feed to a farm in Streidelsdorf that had once been a Polish nobleman's manor. He made us promise that if anyone stopped the cart and found us, we would say we snuck into the cart ourselves and he didn't know anything about it. This Polish man saved our lives. His name was Bolek and he later wanted to marry me.

Bolek got us into the manor and hid us in one of the barns. He brought us shliskes (a dish of flour, potatoes, and onion made into a long log and sliced into pieces). I didn't eat it but Basha couldn't stop eating it. She got sick and Bolek was so nice that he emptied her dirty pails of diarrhea.

It was probably late February when I began working on the farm and I was there for about six months. It had once been a beautiful place with orchards and big fields, a former estate for a Polish nobleman. There were thirty-seven or so Polish and Ukrainian people working on this estate with six hundred prized cows. I milked the cows and made salami. Basha cleaned the cow poop because she wasn't able to manage milking the cows. No one on the farm knew that we were Jews—we were known as the Black Irina and Wanda. I spoke a perfect Polish but Basha spoke a poor Polish with a Yiddish accent. They were suspicious that Basha was Jewish even though she was blond and blue-eyed. I went to church with the workers every Sunday and wrote letters for them in Polish. They were all really nice and respectful to me.

The Russian army soon took over the area and occupied the farm. The people living in the area loaded up their wagons and freed their animals and fled before the Russian advance. There were cows and pigs roaming all over the streets and the houses were emptied. Some people tried to run away using the train, but the railroad tracks were bombed by the Russian advancing army.

We stayed on the farm as much as possible because it was dangerous to be near anyone. The Russians were very rough, especially with the girls. They molested whoever they could. Every night the Russians said, "All of the houses are ours and the girls belong to us."

We heard about three women who were being molested by Russian soldiers and were now hiding out in an abandoned house not too far away. The Polish workers talked about whether they should sneak them onto the farm, but in the end we were too afraid that the Russian soldiers would come looking for them and then molest us. I realized that they were the girls who had abandoned us at the flour mill. I had mixed feelings because I felt bad for the two younger girls but not the older woman who had left Basha and me alone in the forest. The older woman was to blame for the situation now because she had invited the Russian soldiers into the house, hoping to make some money off them.

I had to take care of an errand for the farm and left the estate by myself. Three Russian soldiers saw me walking alone and began running after me. I was afraid they would molest me, so I ran into an empty house and jumped out the second-floor window into the cow dung below. The cow dung saved me and I only broke my leg and cut my head and face. I crawled out of the pile of cow dung, muddy and disgusting, dragging my broken leg. I wanted to drown myself in the river. A different Russian soldier helped me and took me to a hospital in Neusalz where they put my leg in traction. They locked me in the hospital room to protect me from being raped by the Russian soldiers. The Russians were crazy and all the women were in constant danger.

We were very close to the German border and there were so many different people running in all directions in fear from each other. The Russians sent the German people away from the farm and they also were sending the Polish people away. They wanted us girls to chase the cows to Russia on foot. There was no way that I was going to Russia.

I knew what I wanted to do—I wanted to go home to Sosnowiec and see if anyone was alive. I wrote a letter to Rogalski, the apartment superintendent at Targowa 21, to let him know that I, Mira, the Black Irina, was alive and where I was and to please tell anyone who came to look for me. I never received a letter back. I later learned that it had taken months for him to receive my letter; it first went to Russia and then was sent back to Poland.

I needed to get identification papers to have proper ID. I couldn't go anywhere without them and I didn't even know where to go. I wasn't sure if it was safe to leave the area near Breslau (Wrocław). Chaos was everywhere; no one was in charge.

I was determined to get ID papers so I could leave and look for my family. The Russians occupied the area and I begged the Russian general who was in charge to make up papers for me. He refused and I cried and begged without stopping. He kicked me out of his office, but I wouldn't give up. I went back and begged and argued with him more. I knew it was dangerous to fight with him, but I was desperate. The Russian general finally relented and asked me for the date. It was May 20 and I misunderstood his question and gave him that date. That was how May 20 became my official birthday instead of my real birthday, November 29.

## Henry Finds and Rescues Me

It was the summer of 1945; the war had ended but fighting still raged on. I had sent a letter home months ago to let people know I was alive but never received an answer. My location was dangerous because of the population shifting from one area to another. It was not safe to travel, especially as a woman. I didn't have any news about who had survived and if anyone had survived. I wasn't sure what to do.

Henry was freed from his Death March in April. He returned home to see if anyone had survived. He went from his hometown of Siewierz to Będzin and then to Sosnowiec and all the other surrounding neighborhoods. He kept coming back to Targowa Street to check to see if I or anyone from my family had survived. Girls who returned from my camp told him that I had been shot to death on the Death March trying to escape. He didn't give up hope and kept returning to my house. My letter finally arrived and

Rogalski, the superintendent, gave it to Henry because no one else had come back.

Henry decided to come and get me and make sure I was truly alive. Travel was difficult and dangerous, as there was still fighting going on. There were no trains, no buses, and the roads were a mess. He wore a green type of uniform to look like a soldier for safety reasons and set out. He took a picture of himself in this uniform and wrote in Polish on the back of the photograph, "For your memory—to my lovely Mirce," dated June 6, 1945, Będzin. Henry also wrote a letter to accompany the picture—he never sent either but kept them in his pocket until he finally met me. All these years later, I still have the original picture along with his love letter.

*Będzin, 16.6.1945*

*Mirka,*

*I am availing myself of the present opportunity to write you a few words. Firstly, I must tell you that I have received your letter and read it with great joy. You can imagine the happiness I felt when I collected your letter. On account of this letter, I immediately opened a liter of vodka and we drank "l'chaim"; we will have a proper frolic when you arrive. The letter I am writing to you is now the third. I wrote two letters to you immediately after reading yours; you did ask for an immediate response and so I responded immediately. I did not stop there, but set out to come to you, however, I went in the wrong direction and I had to turn back. I was on the road for eight days and I had to return. I no longer know what to think about the fact that you have been free for nearly five months and yet, somehow, I cannot bring you home—I do not mean here, to me, but to the city where you were born and where you grew up. So many people are arriving when they were liberated only a few weeks ago. They come, and you do not. I cannot understand. Different thoughts come to mind. Whenever I am walking in the street, people stop me and ask when you are coming. It is high time you came back. There is nothing new with me. You do not have to worry about me. I am healthy and doing well, I am missing only you. I will leave it at that. I await you with impatience and gladness. I am sending you a picture of how I look now. I give you my warmest regards; all my friends and acquaintances say hello. Regards also from [Hanka Banker], who was with you in the camp, from her sister, from Hela Rubinsztejn (Hela Wilder) and Miss Gliksberg.*

*From me, the ever-faithful Jechiel Rozenblatt, greetings also from my friend Margolies.* [27]

## Love and Freedom: 1945

I left the farm to get bread from a bakery with another worker when news came that there was a strange man in a uniform holding a letter in my handwriting. The people on the farm said, "An American soldier is here and is holding a letter from you and you need to go back to the farm." I was afraid of who this man in a uniform with my letter might be. I didn't know if I was going to be arrested or what was going to happen. I was afraid to walk back to the farm and thought about running away and hiding. I was still acting as a Polish girl and no one suspected me of being Jewish.

Henry scared everybody in his fake uniform. The Russian soldiers were afraid of him because they thought he was an American soldier and the Polish people were afraid because he looked so official. I was very afraid—I had no idea who was wearing a uniform and looking for me and had my letter in their possession. I thought I was going to be arrested.

Before I could run away and hide, Henry met Basha and she told the others to go get me quick and that all was good. I came back to the farm and there was Henry! There we were, standing in the farm, and I was looking at Henry and Henry was looking at me. It was a beautiful moment and I was so lucky.

It had taken Henry many weeks to find the farm and get to Streidelsdorf, but he did. The first time he tried to find the farm he had to turn back because he was totally lost. He set out again with his love and determination to find me and this time, in August 1945, we were reunited. I couldn't believe it. I was so happy to see him! It was like a dream, a true love story.

---

[27] This letter was translated from Yiddish script into Polish and then into English in March 2020.

## Returning to Sosnowiec and Marriage

The next day, Henry and Basha and I began our journey back home. [28] As we walked home, we passed different concentration camps and work camps. I got sick and landed up in the hospital in Grünberg, the town of my former labor camp. I was treated like a regular patient by the medical staff. While I was in the hospital, Henry loaded up a wagon with goods from all of the deserted houses. (This area was in the middle of a land swap among the Polish, German, and Russian people.) After I got out of the hospital, the three of us continued to Sosnowiec with our loaded wagon. A group of Polish soldiers confiscated the wagon and all those goods when we were on the road. My husband always told this story this way: "I started out as a poor man without anything and then I became a rich man with my loaded wagon of goods, and then in a minute I was poor again. But I was not poor. I was wealthier than I ever imagined during all those dark years under the Nazis. I was breathing free air, I saw the daylight, and I had my Mira, alive and with me."

Our first stop was Sosnowiec so I could see for myself if anyone had survived. The Germans were all gone now. I went from house to house looking for anyone; to my house, my aunts' and uncles' homes, my friends'. There was no one, no one at any of these places. There were many rumors about what had happened to all the people who used to live in these houses but no real news. My whole life was gone and everyone with it.

I came to my aunt Rushka's big house, where I met Henry long ago in the stairwell in 1941. I thought back to all that had happened. I realized that I helped save Henry then and now he had saved me. I knew then that we were meant to be together and I was lucky.

The people living in Rushka's house wanted me to show them where the valuables were hidden. I showed them the fine-quality fabric from my aunt's

---

[28] Basha and I remained lifelong friends. Our good friend Margolies fell in love with her and wanted to marry her while we were in Regensburg. Basha thought he was too old for her and married Morris Glauberman. Unfortunately, Basha couldn't have children because of the physical damage from the war and Morris treated her very badly. There was a saying that described these marriages: "Hitler was their matchmaker." Basha was a beautiful girl but she had a bitter life.

haberdashery hidden under the wooden floorboards. I was happy to see that the fabric had been ruined by their constant floor washing and they weren't going to benefit. They had something valuable for me though, my aunt's family album that had been buried in the garden. They sold me the pictures and kept the leather album. I knew I had received a true treasure. I had pictures of my parents, grandparents, and other family members. I couldn't believe once again how lucky I was. The photographs showed our life before the Nazis when we were once just people. People who laughed, cried, married, had children, buried grandparents, went on vacation, and just lived normal, everyday lives as humans.

I didn't know what happened to my family, but that wasn't 100 percent true anymore. I knew that they were most probably dead, but I didn't know for sure and I didn't know any details. That uncertainty ate at me. I needed to know whatever I could about what happened to my mother, my father, Vita Malka, Estusha, Natan, Manek, Herschel, and all of my aunts and uncles, cousins and friends.

Henry and I met every returning train and we shouted out, "Anyone from Sosnowiec? Będzin? Any Rosenblatts? Any Lenczyckis?" There was always hope that someone would return alive or that there would be someone who had seen our family members and give us information about what had happened to them. We looked for any relative who survived and these distant cousins became part of our close family circle no matter where they emigrated to later on.

On one train coming from Russia, I got lucky and my two brothers, Herschel and Manek, answered our shouts. They had survived in Uzbekistan. It was a joyous reunion. I knew I was lucky. My husband, Henry, had no one who survived—not one family member.

Herschel came back married to Eva. Manek wasn't married so he stayed with Henry and me and we were very close. One time, Manek and I snuck into the convent in my old neighborhood of Stary Sosnowiec to get out a little Jewish girl who had been hidden there during the war. This little girl's mother was Manek's good friend and our neighbor. She was part of the Epstein family who lived on Warszawska 10 and had a furniture store. She gave her little girl to the nuns for safekeeping right before she and her husband were arrested. She survived but her husband didn't. When she came back to get her daughter, the nuns told her that the little girl had died. We recognized the little girl when the young girls walked to prayers early in the morning. I jumped over the wall, grabbed her, and threw her to Manek on the other side. The girl didn't cry and went with me willingly. The mother and daughter left Poland and went to Regensburg immediately; they ultimately moved to Israel.

Henry had an apartment in Będzin and we lived there. There were many more Jews living in Będzin than in Sosnowiec. I went back and forth to Sosnowiec regularly to check to see if any other family members or friends survived, but I was afraid to live there. I was afraid the Polish people might remember me as a fighter and someone who stood up for herself and that they would want to get back at me.

Henry helped organize a Jewish Gemeinde (committee) for the survivors as they returned. The committee gave out food, siddurs, and tefillin. Also, there were lists of names to study: names of missing Jews and names of Jews who had survived. Those lists were so much more important than food. It was almost a physical need to learn about who might be alive and even to learn for sure who was dead. [29]

Henry and I got married on the evening of October 2, 1945, immediately after Sukkoth. (The date for the Jewish calendar would be registered as October 3 because the ceremony took place after sundown.) Rabbi Parasol married us but we had trouble finding paper and ink to write a kosher ketubah, the Jewish marriage certificate. Henry ran around and scrambled together enough paper and ink, but it wasn't easy. I still have the original ketubah. Henry also had to scramble to find ten men to be at our wedding.

It wasn't easy for the returning survivors to find a place to live and out of pity we took in an older couple who had lost their son. The woman was bitter

---

[29] One of my cousins, Moshe Rosenblatt, survived, returned to Będzin, and helped with the Gemeinde alongside Henry. Moshe's brother was Hanoch Rosenblatt, who made aliyah in the 1930s. Moshe joined his brother in Israel and lived in Givataim. Despite the distance, our families have remained close all through the years. Moshe and his wife, Tzipporah, and their children, Hannah, Tzvika, and Arye were like a second family to my daughter Lillian when she lived in Israel

and mean and they were jealous of me. I was a new bride and they mocked me because I didn't know how to cook and be a proper wife. I had grown up with a maid and was never interested in doing anything in the kitchen. This couple reported us to the Polish authorities for owning a gun. It was illegal to own a gun, but we had bought a gun on the black market to protect ourselves. Two Polish policemen came to search the house for the revolver. I was sitting on the gun in my bed pretending to be sick. I told them to leave our house and said, "You should be ashamed of yourselves!" They left us with a warning that said if they came back and found a gun, they would shoot all of us.

## Moving to Germany: 1945

Poland was a wasteland. There were still anti-Semitic incidents and even actual pogroms. People were fearful and mistrusting and often cruel. Once Henry and his friend Margolies were on the trolley going to Będzin from Katowice when a Polish man started waving a gun and yelling that he was going to kill any Jews that were left alive. They were scared and jumped off the trolley and walked to Będzin. I was waiting for two hours at the trolley stop for them, getting more and more nervous by the minute.

There was another incident that I remember well. One of our former German neighbors owed my family money from before the war. I came to her and asked for a piece of bread—not the money that she owed. She shouted at me, "They killed all the Jews. How come they left you?"

Many of the survivors wanted to leave Poland once they realized no one else was returning. Very few were willing to stay in Poland with all of the memories and the unrelenting anti-Semitism.

We left Poland and moved to Germany into the American zone, where there was food and assistance for immigration. It was difficult and complicated to travel there. We had to go through Czechoslovakia, even though the German border was right next to our town. We smuggled ourselves into Czechoslovakia, then into Germany, and settled in Regensburg.

## CHAPTER 9

# REGENSBURG, GERMANY: 1945 –1951

Henry refused to live in a displaced persons camp even though many survivors did. He didn't want charity and wanted to be independent. In order to apply for immigration status and for legal status in Germany, we had to get married again, in a civil ceremony. This time, we were part of a group of survivor couples getting married at the same time. It was like an assembly line. The bride wore the wedding gown and held flowers, the groom wore a suit and hat, and the rabbi was there for the ceremony. When one couple finished, the next couple put on the wedding clothes and stood before the rabbi, and so it went on. My wedding pictures were from that second ceremony on January 27, 1947.

Herschel and Manek joined us in Regensburg. [30] Herschel and Eva lived

[30] Regensburg was in the American-occupied zone of Germany and it was filled with survivors. It was a good place to be because there were food and supplies and the US army and other aid organizations to help us restart our lives. We made friends with other survivors from the towns around Sosnowiec and Będzin. The majority of our friends were planning to immigrate to the United States or Israel and were awaiting official immigration papers to come through. No one was planning to stay in Germany or Poland. We found two more cousins

on Landshuterstrasse and they soon had a baby boy named Solomon after my father. I loved this little boy and it was wonderful to see my brother so happy and starting a family. Herschel and Eva immediately applied to immigrate to America through HIAS.

Henry and I were successful in Germany. We opened a small grocery store because it was a business we understood from our childhoods. We made connections with farmers and other stores outside of Germany and began to import fruits and vegetables. The business grew quickly. We soon moved into selling produce as wholesalers to other stores. At that time, food was more valuable than money and we used the produce to barter for other goods and expand the business. We then opened a textile store with my brother Herschel as a minority partner. Henry traveled to inspect and purchase the goods and merchandise and I managed the stores with my brothers Herschel and Manek. I was a hard worker and worked in both stores, and also helped unload the crates of fruits and vegetables from the train when deliveries arrived.

Our first apartment in Regensburg was at Birkenstrasse 11 and then we moved into a nicer place on Maximilianstrasse. Henry learned to drive, and we had a car and sometimes used a chauffeur. There was also a maid in the house. I had a dressmaker who made me the latest fashions, and I accumulated lovely clothes. Everything was so cheap—we bought quality china, linens, and silver.

We were young and happy to be alive. We formed a tight group of friends from fellow survivors and they became our family. In the summer we went to the thermal spas and sanitariums in Bad Kissingen, Mittenwalde, and Garmisch-Partenkirchen to further regain our health and strength. We began to live normal lives.

Germany was still under the United States military in the late 1940s. There was an American army base nearby and we were friendly with many of the soldiers. We were impressed by their kindness and proper behavior. The American soldiers were different from the Russian soldiers. The Russians had

---

who had survived: another Herschel Rosenblatt who emigrated to San Jose, California, and Zavel Rosenblatt, who ended up staying in Germany and moved to Düsseldorf.

been our saviors and were tough soldiers, but they didn't always behave so well, especially with their drinking and wildness with women. The Americans were also tough soldiers, but they were disciplined and helpful. The American soldiers would come over and have coffee and we would talk together and there were times that we invited the Jewish soldiers for Shabbos meals. We bought a carton of cigarettes to resell from a soldier and he saw where we hid our money when we went to pay him. He came back later and stole our money from our hiding place while I was making him a cup of coffee in the kitchen. I was shocked and disappointed when I realized what had happened. Henry and I went to the commanding officer to make a formal complaint, but that soldier's unit had already pulled out of Germany.

We thought highly of the American soldiers and mostly they were very good to us, but there were bad ones among them. Perhaps being a soldier sometimes changed how you behaved. Some soldiers acted as if they could do anything they wanted to and take anything with them before they left Germany.

There was another incident where an American soldier stole something that was important to me. In the summertime, I used to go to the sanatoriums in Mittenwalde, Garmisch-Partenkirchen, and Bad Kissingen. There was a talented German painter named Mason who painted landscapes and portraits. I bought one of his landscape paintings of Mittenwalde that still hangs above my sofa to this day. I liked his work and hired him to paint my portrait. We talked a lot as he painted my picture and I got to know him and saw that he was a nice man. When I came to pick up my picture, Mason was crying. He told me that an American soldier had stolen twenty of his paintings, including mine. These paintings had been commissioned and paid for and he didn't know what to do. It was the end of the summer and there wasn't enough time to repaint everyone's portraits. He wasn't comfortable going to the American commander to register a complaint because he was German. For years, I kept hoping that my portrait would turn up in an art exhibit and I could reclaim it.

I was ecstatic that I was able to get pregnant because during the war years I had no womanly functions. I was nervous, of course, but the pregnancy went smoothly. My daughter, Helena, was born on April 26, 1948. Her birth was difficult, and the German doctor used forceps to deliver her. She was beautiful and we adored her. We named her after my mother. Henry and I were happy and hopeful about life when Helena was born. So many people gushed over her and stopped to admire her that I was afraid of the evil eye. I think that was what happened to her. A woman complimented her so much once when I was in the park that I was uncomfortable and I left. When we got home, Helena started to vomit and got sick and never got better. When Helena was about a year and a half, the IRO (International Refugee Organization) examined Helena for our immigration application in November 1949 and gave us an official stamped document stating that Helena was healthy and a normal baby. However, we were already concerned about her health by the summer of 1949. There seemed to be something wrong with her muscles because she couldn't walk and it was hard for her to hold herself up. The doctors recommended a medicine that only the American Army had access to. I couldn't get hold of that medicine, even with all of my begging and pleading. The doctors next recommended that we go to Switzerland because they might have a special vitamin treatment for Helena. As much as we tried, we could not get visas to go to Switzerland. The diagnosis appeared to be that the German doctor had damaged her head and possibly caused brain damage during the delivery with his forceful use of the forceps. I don't know to this day exactly what it was. And in the end, at twenty-two months of age, on February 26, 1950, at 3:30 p.m., my firstborn beautiful daughter passed away.

Once Helena died, our immigration application had to be amended as we were now only two people. I was extremely depressed and didn't want to leave Germany anymore. I didn't want to emigrate and leave Helena in the ground in Furth. I didn't want to do anything. I lost my will to fight and got sick. Many of our friends had left Germany by this time and we were alone to face our tragedy. Life was bitter. Nothing mattered—not our financial success or our pretty apartment.

Henry decided that we had to leave Germany and Europe immediately and forever. Once Henry made the decision and revised our application, we had to move out of our apartment and move into special housing to await availability on the next US military ship.

We liquidated most of what we owned—our apartment and businesses—as we prepared for final approval and boarding permits for the ship. In the meantime, there were complications: my husband had a black lung from when he worked in the coal mines at Auschwitz and his medical records were holding up our final approval. Tuberculosis was widespread in Europe after the war, so a black lung was a big deal. I went to Munich and pleaded with a doctor there to give me someone else's lung X-rays. This doctor was so nice—he heard me and, without hesitation, gave me another man's X-rays to substitute and wished me luck. Then the German government argued that we owed them taxes. We made a deal with the German government on payment and left one of the stores for my brother Manek to manage and prepared for our departure. We got our final approval and boarded the USS *General R. M. Blatchford* just as our exit permits were expiring.

It took two weeks to cross the Atlantic Ocean and I was sick the whole time. We landed in New York Harbor on January 31, 1951. I was so sick that an ambulance met us at the pier and took me to Beth Israel Hospital. Nothing was working out like we had planned and, as before, we had to start all over again.

Henry in his 'uniform', June 1945

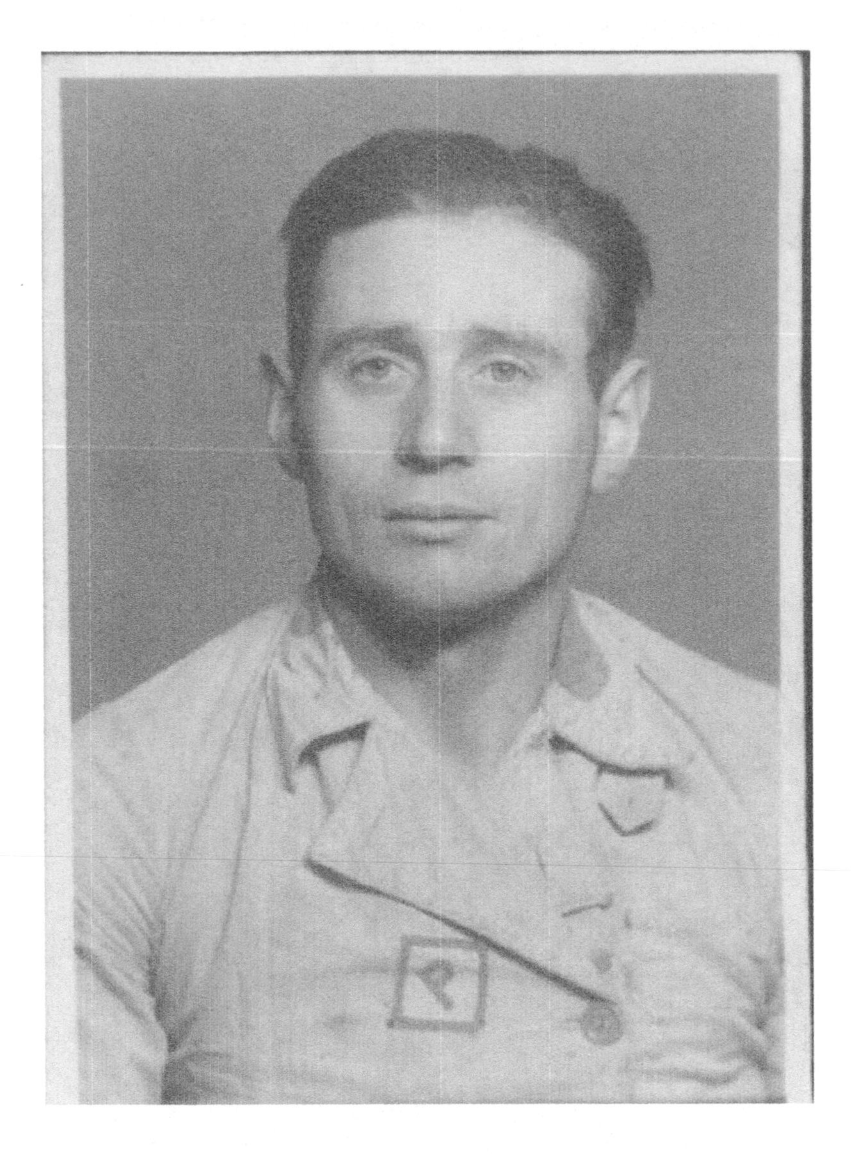

Bolek, Streidelsdorf, Poland 1945. The Polish man who helped me after my escape from the Death March. He has the letter 'P' on his shirt for 'Polish'

My girlfriend, Hanka Banker Appelbaum, Będzin 1945. (She was with me when I first saw Henry and in KL Grünberg. Survived and emigrated to Israel)

My girlfriend, Basha Naigelbauer Zauberman, 1948. (She escaped with me from the Death March. Survived and emigrated to Brooklyn)

Me, Będzin September 1945

My cousin, Zauvel Rosenblatt, me, Henry, Eva and Herschel, Będzin 1945

Basha, Margulies, me, Henry, and Olek Monka, Będzin, October 11, 1945

Henry, Margulies, Olek Monka, Katowice, Poland 1946

Henry, 1946

Henry and me, Regensburg 1946

Henry and my wedding picture from our civil ceremony,
Regensburg January 27, 1947

Henry and me, Regensburg 1947

Me at the Sanitarium, Bad Kissingen 1947

Me at the Zugspitz, 1947

Henry and me, Bad Kissingen 1948

Henry and Manek in front of our store, Regensburg 1947

Henry and me with our first child, Helena, Regensburg 1948

Helena's grave in Furth cemetery, Germany 1950. L to R: Abram Lenczycki married to Lisel and brother of Simon from Australia; Herschel Rosenblatt, cousin, married to Genia, emigrated to San Jose, California; my brother, Manek; Lisel Lenczycki, Genia Rosenblatt; me; Henry

Dinner party with friends, Regensburg 1949. I'm seated at the end in white shirt next to Henry

My passport picture, 1949

Signature of holder
Unterschrift des Inhabers
Rosenblat
COMMITTEE FOR DISPLACED JEWS FROM CONCENTRATION CAMPS
(Siegel)
The president
Der Präsident
Jakob Gottlieb.
5 Februar
Regensburg, den ........................ 1946

My Identity Card #346, Committee for Displaced Jews from Concentration Camps, Regensburg 1946

Anmeldebescheinigung.
Herr Heinrich Rosenblatt
2.8.19.
Regensburg Max – straße Nr. 24/II
hat heute den Betrieb des nachstehenden Gewerbes angemeldet:
Großhandel mit Obst und Gemüse, sowie Südfrüchten. –
Regensburg, den 21. Jan. 1948
Stadtrat
Im Auftrage:
Dieser Schein ist bei Beendigung des Gewerbebetriebes
23827 2M. VIII. 47. N/0608

Registration Certificate for Heinrich Rosenblatt for his Wholesale Tropical Fruits and Vegetables Store on Maxstr. 24/11, Regensburg

# PART II:

# AMERICA

# CHAPTER 10

# NEW YORK

## Coming to America

I arrived in America on January 31, 1951, as a scared, sick, and pregnant new immigrant and Holocaust survivor. After so many years of planning, Henry and I never imagined that our first night in New York would be spent with me in the hospital and my husband sleeping on the stairs by the Wanamaker Store on Fourteenth Street.

I realized I was pregnant shortly after we were approved for passage across the Atlantic Ocean on the USS *General R. M. Blatchford.* We decided to leave as planned because I was determined not to give birth to another baby in Germany. We had missed an earlier opportunity to leave when Helena died and we didn't want to delay our departure again.

It was a difficult pregnancy and I spent the whole trip vomiting and bleeding. I was scared to death that we might lose another child and didn't know what G-d had in store for us. A kind Yiddish-speaking doctor took care of me for the six weeks I was at Beth Israel Hospital and promised that

I would have a healthy baby.

In the beginning, Henry stayed with me in the hospital and then he moved into a dormitory run by HIAS (Hebrew Immigration Association Society). Unlike many of the survivors, we didn't emigrate to the United States through HIAS. We came through our own means because we had time to establish ourselves in Germany.

We arrived with some money and two large crates filled with all kinds of beautiful things like Rosenthal china, Meisner statues, silver tea sets and trays, cut-glass crystal, Shaffenhausen watches, a Leica camera, my treasured painting, as well as the torn green sweater from Helena's shiva. I still have these valuable items, but not the money we saved to help us start our new lives—we lost it soon after we arrived. We thought we had planned well for our move but, unfortunately, it wasn't that simple or easy.

Henry visited his uncle Chil, his father's brother, the day after we arrived. The uncle was Henry's only immediate family member to survive the Holocaust, having left Będzin for Germany and then London before the war. Uncle Chil emigrated to New York right after the war and lived on the Upper West Side with his wife and five daughters. It was wonderful for Henry to sit and talk with his uncle; they shared family stories and talked about who had survived. His uncle was already established in America and had a growing real estate business. Henry gave him our savings of $25,000 to hold but, unfortunately, we made a bad investment decision and lost all of it.

Henry was running around in circles, looking for work and an apartment while learning the city and the language, all by himself. He went to night school to learn English at Washington Irving High School. I saved his black-and-white marbleized school notebook where he wrote, "I will not chew gum in class," one hundred times, after being punished by his teacher. It was ridiculous to think that after all he had lived through, he was forced to do this silly exercise.

We were truly immigrants when we came to America. We didn't know the language or the culture and didn't realize what it meant to be an immigrant. There were many surprising humiliations that we had to go through until we could establish ourselves.

## Washington Heights, New York, 1951–1953

After a few weeks, I was well enough to leave the hospital but had to remain on partial bed rest throughout my pregnancy. Henry had found a lovely apartment in Washington Heights at 94 Wadsworth Terrace. My Yiddish-speaking doctor had an office nearby in the uptown branch of Beth Israel Hospital. I gave birth to a healthy and beautiful baby girl on August 9, 1951. We named her Lillian, after my husband's grandmother, Leah.

Lillian was as good as gold and we felt blessed that she was a healthy baby, but I had a hard time recovering from the birth. I struggled to regain my strength and finally the doctor recommended that I take these atomic isotope injections and drinks to increase my liver and energy levels. The use of radioisotopes and nuclear medicine was new and expensive. It was considered to be a miracle drug and not easily available. My doctor helped make it more affordable and charged us $200 for three doses instead of $200 for each dose. I remember the exact cost because it was so expensive for us at the time. I got half a glass to drink each time and eventually got better. I always think of this as my own personal miracle drug.

It wasn't easy to be a new mother, alone without family and not knowing English. I had always used my ability to speak different languages to protect myself and it frightened me not to be able to do that now. I hated not being able to speak or understand English and I worked hard to learn it as quickly as possible. I made friends with a wonderful older German-Jewish couple, Friedel and Sigmund (Siggy) Guggenheimer, and they became my surrogate parents. They were helpful and caring as I slowly regained my strength and confidence. I loved them and they loved me. I made other lifelong friends in Washington Heights: Henya and her husband Moshe Gerkowitz. Nobody could make Henry laugh more than Henya.

Life in America in the 1950s was a time of safety and security. I used to sit at my third-floor window and watch Lillian sleeping in her carriage in front of the building. We didn't lock our doors and Lillian went back and forth to the Guggenheimers' apartment, eating her favorite food—pickles. Siggy was the manager in Guggenheimer Pickle Company and always brought home lots of pickle jars. Friedel loved taking care of Lillian and she was always sending me off with my girlfriend Henya to shop. I told Friedel I had no money to shop and her response was, "What's wrong with window shopping?" On hot summer nights, we slept in Fort Tyron Park. I was confused the first time I saw people carrying chairs and mattresses to the park.

Henry found work in a factory in the garment center. Although he was a hard worker, Henry kept getting fired because he refused to work on the Sabbath. Henry finally found a job as a cutter for $18 a week. His boss accepted that he wouldn't work on Saturdays but fired him in September when he took off for the Jewish High Holidays and Sukkoth.

Henry knew that he had to find a different line of work. His uncle Chil gave him a job as a housepainter in New Jersey. It took Henry two hours each way to travel to the job by train and bus. Henry was determined to be more than a housepainter or factory worker. He had always been able to look after himself. After the war, Henry had opened three successful stores in Germany without help from anyone. And before the war, he didn't think about making a living because he was studying to be a rabbi and had been accepted to a prestigious yeshiva, Chachmei Lublin.

I tried to make some extra money by working at home while taking care of Lillian. I started to work for a man who imported raincoats from Israel. He told me that if I knew how to sew, he would give me work. I bought a secondhand sewing machine and hemmed the raincoats, getting paid by the piece. It was a struggle to make a living and many times I didn't have money for food. Once I called Henry's family and asked them for $100—I had a plate with four apples on it and nothing else. Nobody realized we didn't have food to eat except the Guggenheimers, who quietly brought us their "extras."

My brother Herschel and his wife Eva had settled in Springfield, Massachusetts, through HIAS when they emigrated to America a few years before us. HIAS had placed several Holocaust survivors there and they formed a close community. My brother made a living selling merchandise to the large non-Jewish Polish-speaking community that lived in the Springfield area. Henry decided to try to see if this could work for him as well.

Henry bought a maroon car with $200 he borrowed from his uncle, loaded it up with basic household needs, including clothes and foods like herring and pickles. He drove through the small towns peddling his goods, using his Polish to speak to his customers who were mostly farmers and factory workers. He stayed in Springfield Monday through Friday and I was left alone in Washington Heights with Lillian. Friedel and Siggy came by every day to check on me and help. Henry came home for Shabbos and spent Sundays on the Lower East Side restocking the car before setting out again.

Henry did this for six months before deciding that we should move to Springfield. Lillian was about eighteen months old at the time. It was hard to leave Friedel and Siggy, but I was excited to be moving near my brother Herschel and his family.

# CHAPTER 11

# SPRINGFIELD, MASSACHUSETTS: 1953–1968

## Settling In with Family and Friends

Our first apartment in Springfield was on White Street next to the shul, Kesser Israel. We then moved to a furnished apartment on 167 Prospect Street in the North End area near my brother Herschel and Eva and their two boys, Solomon and Joseph. Soon after Henry and I moved to Springfield, Herschel and I brought over our brother Manek from Germany. I now had my closest family living in Springfield. I was hopeful that Henry and I could build a happy life here.

My brothers and I were grateful to be together and enjoyed the closeness but, unfortunately, it didn't last because Manek was a changed person. He had trouble finding his way after the war and it got worse over time. He came to America angry, anxious, and secretive. I had always been close to Manek, even when we were children, and Henry and I tried to help him in Regensburg after the war. Our initial immigration applications to America and Israel included Manek and his girlfriend, Tzipporah Altman. Tzipporah couldn't get her visa approved because she had tuberculosis. Manek decided to marry her and stayed in Germany. He moved into our old apartment and managed our remaining store, which in the end failed, as did his marriage. Manek wrote and told us he was desperate to come to America and begged us to help him. Of course, we did everything we could to bring him to Springfield.

Manek moved in with us and I got him a night job at the Westinghouse Refrigerator Repair factory. Our apartment was small and the three of us shared the same bedroom. Henry and I slept there at night and he slept there during the day. Manek was not easy to live with. He was nervous and moody and had no patience for Lillian, who was a little girl who played during the day and made noise. He never gave any money for food or rent, even though he earned a decent salary. He didn't respect that Henry and I were religious and kept Shabbos and kept kosher. Another sore point was that neither Manek nor Herschel wanted me to tell them details about what happened to the family after they ran away to Russia in November 1939. It put a strain on the relationship, and it was a difficult position for all of us.

Our relationship fell apart when I discovered that Manek was living a secret life. He had married a non-Jewish German woman and helped her emigrate to Springfield and used us as sponsors. I only discovered this when I needed Manek's help after Henry had been in a bad car accident coming home from New York on a snowy wintery night. I couldn't reach Manek and when I finally did, he made no effort to help because he was with his wife. This was how I found out what was going on. I was hurt and bitter about his behavior and lies and we became estranged. Thankfully, we reconciled later in life and were able to celebrate many happy family events together.

My uncle Abram was the last of our family members who joined us in Springfield. Herschel and I helped arrange for him and his family to emigrate to the United States from Furth, Germany. It was extremely difficult for Abram to get a visa because America was very anti-Communist and Abram was a Communist and worked in the Communist Party in Poland after the war. They arrived around February/March 1961, around the time of the Berlin Crisis. Uncle Abram, Aunt Genia, and their two daughters, fourteen-year-old Helena and six-year-old Mariola, stayed with us until they got settled. Uncle Abram found work as a Fuller Brush salesman and carried his merchandise door-to-door. Genia set up a small alteration business. I did my best to help Helena and convinced the high school to accept her into an accelerated class even with her limited English. Helena was a brilliant student and graduated with a full college scholarship. I was very proud of her.

Henry and I formed a tight group with the other Holocaust survivors in Springfield. We treated each other as family even though we weren't related. I was one of the lucky ones because I did have family, my brothers and my uncle. We got together, gossiped, told Yiddish jokes, and laughed until we cried. We made fun of our mistakes as we became "Amerikaners," and we understood each other's silences and sadness. Many of the survivors had come from religious families but were no longer religious or even believed in G-d. They were always willing to come to a Shabbos or yom tov meal when I invited them and really appreciated that we included them in our seders. After all, they were our "family" and my children always called them "aunt" and "uncle."

## Children

On May 20, 1954, I gave birth to my daughter Belinda Inez, named for my beloved grandmother, Baila Yehudis. According to my legal documents, Belinda and I shared the same birthday—May 20. Every year, I doubled my age because I celebrated two birthdays—a birthday with Belinda and also my real birthday on November 29, which I later shared with my grandson Zev.

This time, I had an easy pregnancy and birth. However, I had nowhere to leave Lillian when I went to the hospital and had to leave her at a Christian orphanage. It broke my heart to send my little two-and-half-year-old girl away. I remember exactly how Lillian looked as she left me in her kelly green coat with a matching hat and big bow in her hair, and in one small hand, she carried her tiny suitcase.

It wasn't easy to manage with two young children and Henry working long hours and traveling. Lillian was a happy child, always laughing. She loved people and everyone loved to play with her. Belinda was a colicky, sickly baby who was always throwing up and was extremely attached to me. She walked early and held on to one end of my skirt and followed me around day and night. As a baby, Belinda had pneumonia, and once she burned herself badly; I was always running to the doctor or hospital with her.

My son, Morton Melvin, known as Melvin, was born December 21, 1958. He was named after Henry's father, Mordechai Menachem, and he carried on the name Rosenblatt for future generations. Henry and his uncle Chil were the only survivors of this branch of Rosenblatts, who were Kohanim. Melvin was the first and only boy born into the family and his birth was a momentous occasion for the entire family. Henry's uncle and aunt and cousins all traveled to Springfield for Melvin's bris. We were honored by their presence and my husband was so proud.

Melvin was a beautiful little boy, always smiling and happy. He was so cute with his curly hair. We all adored him, including his sisters, and spoiled him rotten. Melvin was a big baby, close to nine pounds, and I had a hard time recovering from his birth. I now had three young children to take care of by myself. Henry worked long hours, and once a week he drove to New York to get new merchandise. He left to go to the Lower East Side on Monday mornings around 5:00 a.m. and returned late at night. During the week, he was on the road all day and often didn't get to spend any time with the children.

## Friendships

As a newcomer in America, I constantly felt the loss of not having my parents. Somehow, I met a few special people that became my replacement family and they gave me love and support during those lonely, frightening years. In Washington Heights, I had the wonderful Friedel and Siggy Guggenheimer. In Springfield, our apartment on Prospect Street was near the Jewish old age home and I visited with my kids all the time. I got very close with one lady, Mrs. Levine. She was like a grandmother, a bubbe, to me, although I always called her by her proper name, Mrs. Levine. Mrs.

Levine and another lady came to my house and cooked food for themselves because they hated the food at the old age home.

They taught me how to cook all kinds of special holiday dishes. I once visited Mrs. Levine when she was sick and I saw that no one had brought her anything to eat. I complained and the manager screamed at me and told me that they weren't responsible to feed her if she didn't come to the dining room, and he didn't care if she starved to death. I made a big stink and got the manager fired. I was always trying to fight for other people's rights.

Mrs. Levine came to us for every yom tov and filled our house with love and warmth. I still use her worn machzor on Rosh Hashanah. I promised Mrs. Levine that she would have a proper Jewish funeral and I kept that promise when she died. I hated that she had been at an old age home and I ridiculously made my little girl Lillian promise that she would never put me in one. Maybe it wasn't ridiculous because my children have kept my wishes.

We moved to Sumner Avenue in the Forest Park area, which was a better neighborhood, before Melvin was born. We lived above our landlord, Mr. Katz, who always complained about my children and didn't make it easy for me. My next-door neighbors, an older couple, Aurore and Alfred LeFebvre, were unbelievably nice and immediately adopted me as part of their family. They were devoted to us and helped me with everything. They treated my children like their grandchildren and let them come over at any time. We spent hours sitting by their fireplace in the winter or in their garden in the summer, watching the children play. I liked talking with old people and was always happy to listen to Mame, Alfred's mother. Aurore and Mame taught me how to bake beautiful cakes and how to garden and plant vegetables. The LeFebvres were French-Canadian Catholics and we learned about each other's customs and religion. I loved people and it never mattered what religion or background as long as they were nice.

I met Muriel Kuzmal on the street walking her baby carriage and asked her to help me with Melvin's baby formula. She came upstairs right away and helped me. Muriel taught me how to make formula and many other things about taking care of children. In those days, it took a whole day to prepare formula for the week. One time, Muriel's little boy, Freddy, knocked over the table with all the finished sterilized bottles of formula. I cried from exhaustion as I sat on the floor cleaning up the mess. Muriel and I became close friends even though our backgrounds were totally different. She came from a large Italian Catholic family who lived in the area.

My other close friend was Pauline Boxer, who was a survivor like me. We understood each other perfectly and never had to explain anything to each other. She was a beautiful woman and we both liked to dress nicely. We shopped together for inexpensive clothing, and we enjoyed sewing together. She ate dinner with Henry and me most nights because her husband went to bed early. I was hospitalized twice when Melvin was a baby, and both times Pauline moved into my house with her two children and took care of my family.

I needed the love and help from these close friends because I had many health issues and had no one else to turn to. When the children were very young, I landed up in the hospital twice. I had my top teeth removed because of a massive gum infection and then had to have a hysterectomy. This was a hard time because I was a young woman who liked to look good, and now I felt ugly and old with my false teeth and hormone changes. I forced myself to be strong and not get depressed. I always made sure to look my best, wearing stylish clothes and going to the hairdresser every week.

## Religious Life

Henry and I were truly religious and believed in Hashem and kept all the Jewish laws. We considered ourselves to be Modern Orthodox and were strictly kosher and observed Shabbos and all the holidays. It was very important to us that our religious observance and traditions continued with our children and we made sure to send them to yeshiva. They started at the Lubavitcher yeshiva before we switched them to a Modern Orthodox yeshiva. The classes were very small, sometimes only six children in a class. When Lillian and Belinda got older, we moved them into public school and sent them to Hebrew after-school programs and Melvin stayed in yeshiva. The whole family went to shul every Shabbos and we were active members at our synagogue, Kodimah. The rabbi, Rabbi Weisfogel, and his wife, Bella, became our closest lifelong friends.

I worked hard to make Shabbos and the Jewish holidays special and joyous, like it had been for me when I was a child growing up in Sosnowiec before the war. Every Shabbos, I invited someone who was alone to join us for our Shabbos lunch, just like my mother used to all those years ago. I made a gala "kiddush" in our house on Simchas Torah—and everything was handmade—the girls and I peeled and grated hundreds of potatoes for kugels. On Purim, I baked for a week and then packed up homemade Shelach Manos for the kids to deliver. I was always ready to cook for a family in need.

## Family Life

One day, Henry came home and told me he had bought a two-family house at an auction—sight unseen and without discussing it with me! We had achieved the American dream in less than ten years.

In 1959, we moved into our new home on 23 Westernview Street. It had a big backyard, a large front porch, and a garage. It was larger and nicer than anywhere we had lived. It was on a quiet street filled with families with young children. The families were mostly Catholic and very American; we were the only immigrant family on the block.

I was happy with life as a New England Yankee. We felt safe and successful. I enjoyed all the work that came with owning our own home. I ran a strict house and the children had chores: everyone had to make their bed and clean their room before breakfast, and they took turns setting the table, washing and drying the dishes, hanging and folding the laundry, as well as dusting and vacuuming. I liked things to be done "proper" and I expected the children to do their chores my way—the "proper" way. I was tough and demanded a lot from my children, but I loved them with a full heart and let them know it every single day. I wanted the kids to have fun and enjoy life. I never hung up the phone with any of my children and grandchildren without saying, "I love you," before saying goodbye.

Some of the jobs were fun, like licking the hundreds of S&H Green

Stamps into booklets so I could use them to get deals when I went grocery shopping. The whole family helped with the outdoor jobs and we made it fun to mow the grass, rake the leaves, and shovel the snow.

All these chores and jobs were important, but Henry and I always believed that the children's main job was to work hard in school. School was easy for Lil, difficult for Belinda because she was painfully shy, and not so easy for Melvin. We hired tutors when we couldn't help them with their work due to our lack of formal education in English. We expected them to do their best and even more.

Henry went to the bakery every morning to get fresh bread and I made a home-cooked meal every night and baked for Shabbos. We never ate frozen food or Wonder Bread or cereal. Henry brought back big jars of herring and pickles and other Jewish foods from New York each week. I sent the girls to school with herring sandwiches! Mel was a very fussy eater and ate salami sandwiches for breakfast for years.

I loved to cook and bake and never found it to be a burden. I always said, "I cooked with love and that is why everything tasted so good." I became a real balabosta, after never helping at home in the kitchen when I was a young girl. I learned to be a great baker and made the best "American" apple pie, yeast strudel, nut cakes for Passover, honey cakes for Rosh Hashanah, and cheesecake for Shavuos as well as my Shabbos marble cake and crispy sugar cookies. No one could ever say I was lazy, as many of the recipes were labor-intensive, like stuffed cabbage, my special Passover potato/flanken cholent, and of course my hand-ground gefilte fish. I used to pickle cucumbers and make jams and compotes when Henry was paid in fruit and vegetables by his farmer customers.

Once a friend brought me a live carp to prepare for Rosh Hashanah. It was too early to make the gefilte fish, so I put the carp in the bathtub and left it swimming there for a few days. I didn't realize that Melvin had become attached to the fish. I took the fish out of the bathtub early one morning and made my gefilte fish. When Melvin got up and saw that the fish was gone, he cried and called me a murderer. The worst part was that it was a tradition to eat a fish head on Rosh Hashanah and I gave my husband the head at dinner.

We didn't think about the kids' sensitivities then like we do now. Melvin probably didn't eat fish for the next fifty years.

I even found time to do things I enjoyed, like gardening and sewing. I discovered I had a green thumb and filled the house with plants. I was proud of my beautiful special rose bushes that needed to be wrapped in burlap and kept indoors in the winter. Everyone I knew seemed to have a sewing machine and sewed their own clothes and I made dresses for the girls and myself. I really loved sewing and took advanced sewing classes at night. Our dining room table was covered with material and McCall's and Butterick patterns during the week. I sewed some of Lillian and Belinda's nicest dresses, and even suits and coats for myself. I always got compliments on my clothes and was proud of my fashion sense.

I was an active mother and loved playing with our children. I took them ice-skating on the pond while Henry waited in the car with thermoses of hot chocolate. I played in the snow with them, making snowmen and snow caves until we ran out of dry clothes. When it snowed at night, I woke them up to make snow angels in the fresh snow. We raked the fall leaves into big piles and jumped in them. We picked flowers and berries, colored, cut out paper dolls, and sewed clothing for their dolls. We made fun birthday parties in the yard for Lillian and Belinda. Melvin loved building things and was always experimenting and trying to blow things up. My children played, and fought, together all the time—that was the way it was. We had fun with everything. One summer, their favorite plaything was an empty cardboard refrigerator box that they used for all kinds of imaginary games until it fell apart. It was a magical time.

One thing I remember well was the disaster with Belinda's hair. Belinda had very long, shiny black hair that everyone admired. One Saturday night, I washed her hair and the hair turned into a rock on top of her head. I couldn't untangle it and after working on it for hours, we drove to my hairdresser and he cut her hair off an inch from the scalp piece by piece. We checked the shampoo and discovered it had glue in it. We tried to sue Palmolive, but nothing came of it. I don't know why, but I've kept Belinda's mass of tangled hair all these years.

We were all big readers. We had English and Yiddish papers in the house and each of my children had a library card. In the summer, the girls would go to the library twice a day to take out books. We listened to the news all the time. The radio was always set to a news station and we watched television network news every night. We didn't know that there would be a time of twenty-four-hour cable news stations that we would have on in the background day and night.

In 1961, the Eichmann Trials were televised, and I watched them every day. It was hard to listen to all the testimony because it seemed even more unbelievable after all these years that I had actually lived through it. I made Lillian and Belinda watch with me when they came back from school. I spoke to my kids about the Holocaust all the time and made sure they knew what had happened. I also made the kids watch the news when, in 1965, Pope Paul VI forgave the Jews for killing Jesus.

Sunday night was family television night and that's how we learned about history and American culture. We ate our supper watching The Twentieth Century narrated by Walter Cronkite, the newscaster. Then we moved to the living room and watched The Ed Sullivan Show, a variety show with all kinds of entertainment. My husband loved watching whenever the Beatles were on because of the crazy fans. He thought it was the funniest thing, it was so different from anything he had experienced.

We had lots of good times when the children were growing up. Henry loved swimming and every summer we rented a house near the water. In the early years, we went to Moodus, Connecticut, but soon we spent every summer in Old Lyme, Connecticut, where Herschel and his brother-in-law Moshe owned a cottage. We rented a house for a month and spent every day at the beach with our extended family of survivors. Over the years, we became a large group that included Herschel and Eva and their boys, Solomon and Joseph; Moshe and his boys, Joey and Lee; Abram and Genia and their girls, Helena and Mariola; Chana and Manny, and their children, Steven and Rita. Sometimes my good friend Pauline Boxer came with her family. We sat on the beach from morning to sunset. Henry taught all the kids to swim and they played together all summer long. At night, the adults would sit around drinking tea, laughing, and playing cards—kuten shpleering—while the kids ran around catching fireflies. Sometimes the whole group piled into two cars and went to a drive-in movie. On Sunday mornings, I took the kids and we filled their sand pails with blueberries and then I made blueberry pancakes for breakfast. Those were such fun times.

We used to spend a few weeks in Saratoga Springs in the summer so I could take the mineral bath treatments for my arthritis. We went as a family and stayed in inexpensive rooming houses with other survivors. From there we took road trips to Lake George, Lake Champlain, Thousand Islands, Fort Ticonderoga, and other New England historic sites. Henry loved to drive and was always willing to go somewhere new.

I went to Saratoga Springs in the summers and to Hot Springs in the winters for my arthritis. Both areas had famous horseracing tracks and twice a year I spent time with a group of gentlemen who were involved in that world. They were very lively and so different from anyone I ever met before, but they treated me with great respect and we became friends. They used to sneak my girls into the racetrack and let them sit up high on the reviewing posts to watch the races.

Friends and a sense of community were always important to me. In Springfield, I had my family, my group of survivor friends, and my shul friends. Our home was open to all and my children's friends were always welcome. The house was always full of people, both children and adults.

## New York General Home Supply Company

After many years of peddling his goods door-to-door, Henry decided to open a store near where many of his loyal customers worked. It was hard for him to be on the road all the time. It was also hard for me to be alone so much of the time with three young children. Henry hoped a store would provide a better income and life for us. The name of our store was the New York General Home Supply Company, known as a "dry goods" store. These types of stores don't exist today. The store was small and packed with goods and we were very proud of it. We sold all sorts of things—small appliances, watches, wallets, belts, linens, and a complete line of clothing for children, women, and men, including hosiery, lingerie, pajamas, and uniforms. As the kids got older and were in school, I started to help in the store; over time, I worked there every day.

The store was located on Sharon Street in the North End where we had first lived when we came to Springfield. Ten years later, it had become a rough neighborhood, filled with empty lots and abandoned buildings. Our first store was a small one-story cement building that was the only structure still standing on the block. We had a loyal worker, Jimmy, and a German Shepherd watchdog named Petty. Jimmy loved and respected Henry and was willing to help us with everything. On the days that Henry went to New York for new merchandise, Jimmy opened and closed the store with me and never left me alone. He then stayed to help us unpack the car late at night when Henry returned.

Many of our customers worked at Fisk Tire and Rubber Company in Chicopee Falls. One Christmas season, the union called for a general strike and the workers were struggling to make ends meet. Those workers were our customers and they had no money for Christmas gifts. We worked out an arrangement where we discounted our merchandise and told them they could pay us just a little bit each month; we had them give us what they could afford. In addition, we made up small packages and gave one to each customer as a Christmas gift for their children. We knew many of our customers and their families personally and were devoted to them, and they were loyal to us.

It was a struggle to make a living. We closed early on Fridays and were closed both Saturdays and Sundays. We thought it would help if we opened the store on Sundays, which was against the law in Massachusetts. The blue laws didn't let businesses open on Sunday, the Christian Sabbath. Springfield was a Catholic city and Henry and I set out to change the law. We decided to sue because the blue laws discriminated against Jewish Sabbath observers. Everyone said, "Look at those Greenhorns. What do they think they are doing?" Some of our friends laughed at our chutzpah and never thought we had a chance to win.

It took years for our suit to go through the courts and we finally won in the Massachusetts State Court in 1964. Governor Peabody signed the Sabbatarian Bill, which allowed store owners to conduct regular store hours on Sundays providing that they observe Sabbath on Saturdays. We now had a permit that allowed us to open our store on Sundays. It was an incredible accomplishment and we were very proud of ourselves. We were recent immigrants with no formal education, Holocaust survivors, who won our rights against the strong Catholic Church in Massachusetts. We were always willing to fight for what we believed was right, no matter how hard or how long. All the local newspapers interviewed us and published our story.

Our customers loved that the store was open on Sunday because it was convenient for them to shop with their families. This extra day helped us make a better living. However, being open on Sunday caused problems at home. Lillian now had to watch Belinda and Melvin on Sundays in addition to watching them during the week until I got home from the store right before their bedtime. It was hard for her to have so much responsibility and Belinda and Melvin made it harder because they didn't behave. As the kids got older, it was hard on me because I worried that all three of them had too much freedom.

Unfortunately, the neighborhood got so bad that it was difficult to keep the store open. There were many Friday nights when the phone rang repeatedly as we sat down to our Shabbos meal, and we knew that once again the store had been broken into. In the end, the state took the store away through eminent domain in the Urban Renewal programs of the 1960s and we received no compensation.

We stayed in the area but moved to Main Street, where there were other small businesses. It was a safer location and our store had display windows. Jimmy remained as loyal as always and our watchdog Petty became our family dog.

## Changes and Leaving Springfield

Life got complicated in 1967–1968. My back went out and I could barely walk. I crawled to the seders that year and after that I was completely bedridden. I needed an operation to remove a disc that was causing my leg to atrophy. The doctors warned me that if the surgery failed, I would probably never walk again. Fortunately, the operation was a success and I slowly recovered.

It was a particularly hard time for my husband. He had a sick wife, children who were growing up and needed attention, and a business to run. The store was not doing well because people were afraid to shop in the area. The neighborhood had further deteriorated and became dangerous. Urban Renewal was preparing to demolish all the buildings on Main Street, like they had done on Sharon Street a few years earlier. Once again, we had to find a new location for New York Home General Supply Company.

Henry didn't want to open another store and have it taken away again. He wanted to make a better living and not be so nervous. We decided to make a big change, leave Springfield, and return to New York. We believed there would be better business opportunities there. In addition, the children were getting older and we wanted to raise them in a more Jewish environment.

Springfield had given us the happy life I had hoped for when Henry and I moved there years earlier. It had been our home and a place where we raised our children and became Americans. We had a house and good friends and were part of a close community. We were successful in providing our children with a safe and easier life, even though we struggled to make a living. And we were successful in raising our children with our Jewish traditions and religious beliefs, even though the Orthodox community was small. It was scary to uproot our lives yet again and start over, but we knew we had to make the change.

In February 1968, we closed the store for good. Henry was fifty years old and he was about to begin a new career. He began traveling back and forth to New York considering different business opportunities. That summer, Henry began working as a diamond cutter on Forty-seventh Street and I began to pack up the house. In September, Lillian left to go to Northeastern University in Boston. It was a time of big changes and everyone was nervous and sad, including Belinda and Melvin, who didn't want to move and leave their friends.

On Halloween night, October 31, 1968, we left our home on 23 Westernview Street, Springfield, and moved to New York.

Me with Lillian, 1951

Henry and me with his cousins Sydney and Helen Schlesinger and their baby Isaac, Washington Heights 1952

Me, Lillian and baby Belinda visiting Friedel and Siggy Guggenheimer, Washington Heights 1955

Henry and me at Mendy Pollack's bar mitzvah in New York. Sitting with Uncle Chil's daughters and husbands, Mutti and Bette Retter, Leah and Leon Eisenberg, Jack and Millie Vorhand, 1955

Henry and me with Manny and Chana Koslowski, 1956

Lillian's third birthday with Henry and me at 167 Prospect Street, Springfield 1954

Belinda and me, Springfield 1955

Henry with Belinda and Lillian who is wearing the green coat she wore to the orphanage when I went to the hospital to give birth to Belinda, Springfield 1955

Belinda and Lillian with me, Moodus, Connecticut 1957

Henry and me with our children, Lillian, Belinda and Melvin on Thanksgiving Day, 23 Westernview Street, Springfield November 26, 1959. My painting from Mittenwalde hangs above the mantel.

My children, Lillian, Belinda and Melvin, 1960

Lillian, me, Melvin and Belinda on a road trip to Thousand Islands, 1966

Henry and me, Hot Springs, Arkansas 1965

Family gathering at 23 Westernview Street, Springfield c. 1965. L to R: Liesel and Moshe Skrzypeck (brother and sister-in-law of Eva Rosenblatt); me; my cousin Simon Lenn from Australia; my sister-in-law Eva and my brother Hershel; my Aunt Genia and my Uncle Abram

Me in the backyard of 23 Westernview Street, 1964

Henry and Jimmy outside New York General Home Supply Company, 1840 Main Street, Springfield 1966

Bus. 736-9636 Res. 734-8354

N. Y. GEN'L. HOME SUPPLY CO.

OPEN SUNDAY

CLOTHES, DRY GOODS, SPORTWEAR AND GENERAL MERCHANDISE FOR THE ENTIRE FAMILY

BUY THE BEST FOR LESS

HENRY ROSENBLATT, PROP.

Henry and me with Lillian in front of our store, 1967

# CHAPTER 12

# BROOKLYN

## Starting Over Once Again

We arrived in Brooklyn on November 1, 1968, and moved into our large apartment on Ocean Parkway, where I have lived ever since. I don't think any of us were prepared for what a change it would be to live in New York. It wasn't easy to move from a house to an apartment and everything around us was so much bigger and noisier. Everything was strange and different and, once again, we had to find our way.

Henry had the easiest adjustment to our move. He liked being part of a large Jewish community and felt more comfortable and secure than he had for all the years we lived in Springfield. He quickly learned how to cut, sort, and grade diamonds and enjoyed working in the diamond business, buying and selling goods on Forty-seventh Street. He had a partner, Abraham Schreiber, and their company was called A. S. & R. Diamond Corp. The business was doing well.

Belinda and Melvin had a more difficult adjustment fitting into Brooklyn.

The yeshivas we were able to get them into were too religious and not for them. At the same time, they were seeing the big cultural changes of the sixties. Springfield was ten years behind the times and none of us knew anything about this culture; the sixties revolution was new to all of us.

It was challenging to be a parent during these years and our recent move just made it more difficult. When Lillian came home from college for that first Thanksgiving, I was in shock to see her hippie clothes and wild hair. She attended sit-ins, demonstrations, and went to Woodstock that summer. It was difficult to understand our children during their teenage years because our teenage years had been so different. Those were our worst years as our worlds fell apart and we struggled to survive. The generation gap between us was enormous and it wasn't easy for Henry and me to figure how to be parents. But we got through them and we stayed very close to our children. They knew that we would always be there for them, even as they got older and made their own ways in the world.

I liked living in Brooklyn, but it took me time to get used to a different way of living. One change was driving, which was very different in Brooklyn than in Springfield. It was scary, especially for me as a nervous driver, but I was determined to continue driving. I had fought hard to get my license, taking the written exam many times because of my poor English. When I finally took the driving test, the tester refused to pass me. He said, "What? Do you think I'd let someone like you pass on the first time?" I'm not sure if he meant because I was Jewish or because I was an immigrant. I reported him to the supervisor, who passed me. I was always willing to fight for my rights, big and small.

While Henry was busy with the business and the children were settled in school, I found I had nothing to do. I decided to look for a job because I needed to be busy. I became a saleswoman in the coat department at Martin's, a family-owned department store in downtown Brooklyn. I worked there three days a week for ten years. I loved working at Martin's and received letters of praise and bonuses. One year the owner personally gave me a $600 bonus because they were pleased with my good work. I treated my customers with respect and honestly told them if the coats looked good on them and had my own group of clients. The other saleswomen were jealous of my work ethic and were mean to me—they were American Jews—they called me "greenhorn" and "shommie"—short for shomer Shabbos because I didn't work on Saturday. They made fun of my accent; they wouldn't help me with the cash register; but they always asked me to figure out the sales tax for them.

Martin's closed in 1979 and I began to help Henry and his partner on Forty-seventh Street. I started to sell jewelry privately and had my own customers. We moved out of our office at 30 West Forty-seventh Street and worked out of the Diamond Club. It was a nice setup to do business and we continued working for many years past retirement, even taking Access-A-Ride back and forth. Henry and I both liked to be busy.

## Success and Good Times

We were happy in New York. Life was much livelier than in Springfield. We were successful in business and had a busy social life. We got closer with Henry's cousins and their growing families. We had a group of fellow survivors from our synagogue, the Young Israel of Ocean Parkway, and we called ourselves the "Continentals." We became the best of friends and vacationed together in Miami Beach and the Catskill bungalow colonies. We took turns hosting Oneg Shabbats on Friday nights, where we showed off our beautiful china and silver and baking skills. I loved being a hostess and never minded all the work.

In the summer of 1970, we decided to take advantage of the cheap airfares and took a family trip to Germany, France and Israel. In Germany, we visited my Aunt Lodja who had remained in Furth. We went to Helena's grave in the Jewish cemetery. It was the first time we had been there since we had left in 1951. Then we spent a few days in Paris before going on to Israel. It was an exciting time to go to Israel, so soon after the Six-Day War of 1967. We felt like kissing the ground when the plane landed because it was such an incredible feeling to actually be in Israel. We went to the Kotel/Wailing Wall almost immediately and prayed for ourselves and for our parents and all the family who never had the zichus/privilege to pray there.

We rented an apartment in Tel Aviv and traveled all over Israel seeing as much as possible. We reconnected with family and friends, Moshe and Gizzie Rosenblatt, the Shiratskys, the Panskis, other Lenczyckis and Rosenblatts. I visited Hanka Banker, my friend who was with me throughout the war; when I first met Henry, in the Sosnowiec ghetto, and Grünberg concentration camp. I also saw Karol Tuchschneider, my friend who smuggled himself to Hungary wearing the Nazi uniform I stole for him. I told him that his sister had been part of a prisoner exchange between Grünberg concentration camp and Denmark late in the war and was buried in Denmark. Night after night, we sat on their balconies and drank tea while we talked about our past lives and told about our new lives. It was the most special of times and it felt wonderful to be alive.

My trip home was dramatic. I flew back to New York through Paris with Belinda and Melvin on Labor Day weekend, September 1970. That Sunday, September 6, Arab terrorists (Popular Front for the Liberation of Palestine) hijacked four passenger planes from Europe to the Middle East. Most passengers had no idea about a terrorist threat but obviously the airlines knew something because our connecting flight was canceled, as were most other international flights. The Orly airport was a madhouse, filled with frantic passengers who didn't understand what was going on. There were enormous lines at the pay phones, very little food left in the shops, and people trying to find a place to sit in the crowded airport. I was there for almost two days, alone with two kids and no money. A lovely gentleman helped me out and told me about the warnings of a possible terrorist attack. The gentleman and I became good friends and for many years he visited me when he was in New York.

We were lucky to finally get on a flight Friday afternoon and landed in New York right before Shabbos. We were so relieved to finally be home and even more relieved when we woke up Sunday morning to the news broadcast about Black September and the hijackings.

In December 1971, we made a gala weekend bar mitzvah for Melvin. It was a Shabbos filled with love and pride as my only son carried on our traditions and heritage. I was surrounded by our closest friends from Springfield and Brooklyn and so many family members from all over. Simon from Australia came with his whole family, as did some of the Israeli cousins. It felt like we had finally won the war and the Nazis had lost.

My husband and I were always willing to stand up and fight for our beliefs. A situation developed in our synagogue where we were forced to stand up for what we believed was right and it didn't end well. Melvin and the other young men in the shul were being treated badly and we fought for changes. The rabbi and board members refused to do anything different and the situation escalated to the point that they called Henry to a Beis Din. It was a very upsetting time and in the end we left and started a new shul with Melvin and his friends called Shaarei Shalom. Sadly, our close friendships with the Continentals were badly hurt by the situation.

## Children Growing Up

My children were growing up and moving in different directions. In June 1972, Lillian married Larry Schwartz, whom she met during her junior year at Hebrew University. They made aliyah in 1975 after Lillian received her master's degree in social work from Wayne State University. I had such mixed feelings about Lillian making aliyah. Henry and I were real Zionists. We supported Israel in all ways and went to the Israeli Day Parade every year until 2016. I was truly proud of Lillian but it was painful to have her so far away. The times were different; phone calls were expensive, and people didn't fly often. We mostly wrote to each other on thin blue airmail paper and made occasional phone calls. Lillian and Larry were successful as new *olim* but were unsuccessful in their marriage. Lillian lived in Jerusalem, working as a probation officer, for over ten years before she returned to New York to be with family.

In 1991, Lillian married Jeff Fischler and they have two sons, Gabriel and Daniel. Lillian has a successful private practice as a clinical therapist in Manhattan and Westchester and Jeff's career has been in financial advertising. Jeff was unfamiliar with our religious lifestyle and had limited knowledge of

Holocaust survivors, but he was always amazingly respectful to Henry and myself. Lillian's passion was adventurous travel and she has traveled the world, finding new and exciting places to visit each year.

Belinda stayed in New York for college and graduate school and received an M.Phil in history from the Graduate Center of the City University of New York. She was an editor/researcher on a long-term Holocaust studies project called the *International Biographical Dictionary of Central European Emigres from 1933 to 1945*. Belinda married her high school boyfriend, Jack Levavi, in 1976. They remained in Brooklyn to raise their three sons: Ruvin, Zev, and Abe. Although history has always been her passion, Belinda became an executive recruiter and has her own company called Sandra Green Legal Placement, Inc. Jack worked with Henry in the diamond business before switching into insurance. Jack's background was similar to ours; he came from a religious immigrant family and his first language was Yiddish. It was easy for us to be around him—he completely understood us and we were very close.

Melvin stayed in Brooklyn for college and medical school and received his M.D. from SUNY Downstate Medical Center. He excelled and had fellowships at Johns Hopkins University and Yale University and became an interventional radiologist. Melvin married his longtime friend and then girlfriend, Sara Einhorn, in 1982. Sara's parents were religious Holocaust survivors who had the same views as we did. My only granddaughter, Danielle is their oldest child, and they have two sons, Jonathan and Matthew. Sara practiced as a nurse for many years and was always willing to come into Brooklyn to help us with our health issues.

Melvin was passionate about medicine and science and always wanted to be a doctor. As a kid, he was fascinated by the Space Program and I think that was what started his love of science. Years later, one of his patients invited Melvin and his family on a private tour of Cape Canaveral and he asked me to join them.

Melvin was co-director of the Vascular and Interventional Radiology Department at Yale before setting up his private practice, Connecticut Image Guided Surgery. Mel became a world-renowned doctor in the area of venous disease and was the president and chairman of the American Vein and

Lymphatic Society, publishing over eighty articles in his field.

The Holocaust was always present in our house and my children were affected by my stories of lost loved ones. I think they chose their careers and interests because of what they experienced at home. They wanted to make a difference and help people in the world. Lillian chose to be a therapist and Melvin to be a doctor. Belinda became the family historian and chose to document the Holocaust.

Melvin, me, Belinda in passport picture, 1969

Belinda, me, Melvin and Lillian on our trip abroad, Germany 1970

Melvin's Bar Mitzvah, 1971. L to R: My brother Herschel; my Uncle Abram; my Aunt Genia; me; Melvin; Henry; cousins Simon and his wife Sara and daughter Marilyn

Lillian, Melvin and Belinda at Melvin's Bar Mitzvah, December 1971

Henry and me at Lillian's wedding, 1972

Me and the "Continentals," 1975

Me at Martin's department store, c. 1977

Henry and me with our first grandchild, Ruvin, 1983

Henry holding Ruvin, Melvin with Lillian on top, Belinda and me, 1984

Melvin's wedding, 1985. Melvin, me, Henry, Lillian, Belinda, Jack and baby Ruvin

Me and my grandsons, Ruvin, Zev and Abe, 1989

Lillian and Jeff's wedding, 1991: L to R: Henry; me; Belinda holding Zev; Jack; Lillian; Jeff; Melvin; Sara; front row, Abe; Ruvin; and Danielle

Me and my relatives at Lillian and Jeff's wedding, 1991: L to R: cousins Marisha and Moshe Danziger; my sister-in-law Eva and my brother Herschel; my Aunt Genia; me; cousins Simon and Paula Raber; my sister-in-law Judy and my brother Manek

Henry and me in Alaska celebrating our 50th anniversary, 1995

My grandchildren, Sackett Lake 1995. L to R: Me holding Jonathan; Henry holding Danielle; Ruvin; Zev holding Gabe; and Abe

Me and my brothers, Manek on the left and Herschel on the right, December 1998

Melvin' family at my grandson Zev's Bar Mitzvah, 1999. Danielle, Sara holding Matthew, Melvin, and Jonathan

My oldest grandson Ruvin and me, 1999

Me with my grandsons Gabe and Danny, 2000

Henry and me with my grandson Abe, Sackett Lake 2000

Me with my only granddaughter Danielle, Saxony Hotel 2005

Henry and me playing shuffleboard with Belinda's family, Abe, Belinda, Zev and Ruvin, Saxony Hotel, Miami Beach c. 1999

Henry and me with Melvin, Saxony Hotel 2005

Family Passover, Saxony Hotel, Miami Beach, 2001. L to R: First Row – Danielle; Abe; and Ruvin. Second Row - Sara holding Matthew; Jonathan; Gabe; Jack holding Danny; Belinda; and Zev. Standing – Melvin; Lillian; Jeff; me; and Henry

Henry and me in Miami Beach, 2003. Henry's Auschwitz number 157756 can be seen on his forearm

My grandson Ruvin and Erika's wedding, 2005. L to R: Jack; Belinda; Ruvin; Erika; me and Henry; Abe and Zev in back.

My grandson Danny's Bar Mitzvah, 2011. L to R: First Row – Danielle; Lillian; Jeff; Danny; Gabe; Jeff's father and partner, Susan and Bill Fischler. L to R: Second Row – Sara; Matthew; Melvin; Henry; me; Belinda; Jack

Henry and me with the family. L to R: Jonathan; Daniel; Jack; Danielle; Zev; Melvin; Gabe; Jeff; Danny; Belinda; Sara; Lillian; Passover 2015.

Henry and me with Lillian and her boys, Gabe and Danny, Passover 2016

Henry in the Passover Tea Room, Ft. Lauderdale 2015

Henry and me at his last Passover, Ft. Lauderdale 2016

# CHAPTER 13

# REMEMBERING THE HOLOCAUST

## Holocaust-Related Events

I had always spoken about the Holocaust and what had happened to me and my family. I spoke to my children, my friends, and my relatives. I spoke to anyone that would listen—it didn't matter if they were Jewish. I felt that it was the best way I could to honor my parents and family, and for many years, I was a lonely voice talking about the past.

My husband and I always went to the Warsaw Ghetto Memorial in New York, first held in Temple Emanuel and later at Madison Square Garden. We took our kids and we even took my oldest grandchild, Ruvin. Henry was one of the few survivors who wore a yarmulke because the religious community was not as active in Holocaust memorials yet.

For many years, Henry didn't talk about his experiences in the Holocaust and neither did my brother Herschel. It was too painful and perhaps they had "survivors' guilt." Very few survivors were comfortable talking about what they had gone through. There was a feeling that nobody really wanted to hear about it; it was the past and better to put our energies into the future. Other Jews said, 'Live your life. What happened happened, and there's no need to feel bad by talking about it." That feeling changed in the 1980s as more survivors began to share their experiences and realized that people were willing to listen.

In 1980, Henry testified at a war crimes trial in Aschaffenburg, Germany, against his SS-Lagerführers, Stefan Olejak and Ewald Pansegrau from the subcamp Jaworzno. We decided that Belinda and Lillian should go with him to be witnesses for the next generation. It was emotionally difficult for Henry to testify in Germany, and one night he had such severe nightmares that he needed medical attention. They went to Helena's grave in Furth and then Henry took the girls skiing to Garmisch-Partenkirchen where we had been in a sanitarium after the war. We heard later that the court acquitted both SS guards because of insufficient proof. The judge claimed that the court could not rely on the memories of the former prisoners, and that the witnesses that were brought from overseas felt pressurized to give the evidence that was expected of them. [31]

In 1986, Henry testified in open court in Germany against Horst Czerwinski, the SS-Unterscharführer in Lagischa, a subcamp of Auschwitz, who was on trial for the execution hanging of five men who had tried to escape. One of the men was his childhood friend, Mendel Zborowski from Siewierz. Henry knew the brutality of Horst Czerwinski only too well because Czerwinski had been the kommandant in charge of two of the subcamps that Henry was assigned to when he was in Auschwitz: Lagischa and Golleschau. Czerwinski then became the column commander for Henry's group on the Death March. Coincidentally, Horst Czerwinski had been the SS commander involved in the liquidation of the Jews in Sosnowiec before being assigned to Lagischa. [32]

---

[31] http://www.tenhumbergreinhard.de/1933-1945-taeter-und-mitlaeufer/1933-1945-biografien-o/olejak-hans.html

[32] My Thesis Harry: The Documented Tribulation of One Auschwitz Survivor, by Daniel B. Burns, MA and Harry Zborowski (#157837). ISBN 978-0-615-72995-4-51695, pp.224-226. In 2004, Henry was contacted by Dan Burns, a historical researcher, regarding this testimony. Dan was writing his doctoral thesis on Mendel Zborowski's brother Chil, who survived the war and lived in Canada. Dan Burns provided Henry with original documents proving the

In 1981, I attended the first World Gathering of Jewish Holocaust Survivors in Israel. I went alone and stayed with Lillian. It was an unbelievable event and I was so happy to be there. I gave testimony at Yad Vashem and filled out forms with names of lost relatives, hoping for a match. In 1983, Henry and my girls and I attended the American Gathering of Jewish Holocaust Survivors in Washington, D.C. Everyone went to these early gatherings hoping to meet someone who had survived or to find out information about loved ones. After these gatherings, more survivors began to talk about their experiences—maybe also because their children, the "second generation," were ready to listen to their stories. We went to many of these organized conferences and reunions and always met people we were surprised had survived. In 1995, the American Gathering of Jewish Holocaust Survivors held a large gathering in New York, commemorating the fiftieth anniversary of our liberation. All my children went with us to the programs.

In 1997, Henry and I were interviewed for the Spielberg Archive for The Institute for Visual History and Education, USC Shoah Foundation. A film crew came to our house to tape our testimony and stayed for almost twelve hours. Henry spoke for eight hours without stopping; it was like a dam had burst open. He had begun to tell the children bits and pieces about his past but this was the first time he spoke about everything he had gone through. After this, he was able and willing to talk to people about his experiences. I found it difficult to talk while they were filming me and kept breaking down in tears. I was disappointed that I didn't do a better job telling my story. I always hoped to redo my testimony and leave a better account for myself, which is why I am writing this book.

---

confiscation of his family's property and stature in Siewierz. Most important, Dan Burns gave Henry the great gift of the names and birth dates of his nieces and nephews. For over fifty years, Henry was tortured because he couldn't remember their names and now, he found peace.

## Holocaust Trips

The first time I went back to Poland was in 1988. It was Melvin's idea to go and he wanted it to be a father-son trip for Henry and himself. Once they started planning it, I couldn't bear not to be part of it and I joined them, along with Sara, Melvin's wife. It was a complicated trip to arrange because Poland was still a Communist country and not many survivors had returned. Everything in the country was strictly regulated; we stayed in certain hotels, used specially licensed guides, and had to change a set amount of money each day. There was no kosher food so we traveled with our own food, salamis, sardines, and nuts. We went to our hometowns of Sosnowiec and Siewierz where nothing had changed over the last forty years. It was the first year of the March of the Living at Auschwitz and the four of us joined the march.

After telling my stories to my children over the years, I was glad to be able to show Melvin and Sara firsthand what my old life looked like. We went to Targowa Street and saw my house, and then found the schoolyard where my transport had taken place. It was a miserable trip for Henry, and he couldn't wait to leave Poland. He was paralyzed with fear and he couldn't remember anything because it was too painful. The best part of the trip for him was joining the March of the Living. It gave him comfort to march with other Jews, singing and dancing with the Israeli flag on Polish soil.

Unfortunately, the trip only got worse. Henry was so tense in the train station that he fell as we boarded the train to Vienna from Poland. In all the commotion, we didn't realize that he had lost his passport until we reached passport control. My son, Melvin, explained the situation and after some time, everyone understood and helped us through this complication.

At Henry's urging, we went back with my daughters, Lillian and Belinda, in September 1997. Poland felt different now because it was no longer a Communist country. It was easier to travel and we hired a personal driver to take us around. We went to our hometowns and other cities as well as our forced labor camps of Grünberg, Lagischa, Golleschau, and Zielona Góra where Henry had found me after the war. Most of our neighborhoods and places still remained the same. When we went back to Grünberg, my old barracks with the skylights was still standing, as was the "hanging tree" in front of it. The director of the factory allowed us to tour the factory and listened carefully as we went from floor to floor as I described the machines and various processes I had worked on. Crazily, the director asked me to be their sales representative in New York and gave me fabric samples. We spent a long time looking for the farm where Henry had come to save me after the war. We kept showing our picture postcard of the manor house, but nobody recognized it. When we finally found the place, we understood why. It was in terrible condition and completely abandoned. Henry and I walked around and thought back to that special moment when we saw each other for the first time after the war.

Henry had a better trip this time because he was less anxious. Very little had changed in his hometown of Siewierz, and this time he was able to remember his house, the street, and the neighbors. A group of elderly ladies were sitting in the square where the shul used to be and remembered him as "the little one who used to get the cholent pot from the bakery on Shabbos morning." The family who now lived in his house had helped his father in their store during the war and let us come in and walk around.

An old woman approached Henry and showed him a chair that belonged to his father that she had saved all these years, waiting for someone from his family to return and claim it. She imitated putting on tefillin and praying and explained that Henry's father had sat on this chair while davening in her house every morning because her house had no windows. We were so touched by this that Henry decided that he wanted her to keep the chair on the condition that she continued to share the story of this chair with her grandchildren and future generations.

We spent Shabbos in Berlin and traveled to Helena's grave in Furth before heading home. We were very proud that we took our children back to see and feel our history before it became common for people to go back.

Henry and I returned to Poland in 1999 to put up a gravestone and memorial plaque for Henry's two brothers, Srulik and Herschel, who were buried in a mass grave with over a hundred Jews in the Jewish cemetery in Zawiercie. According to eyewitness accounts, Srulik and Herschel were shot to death by the Nazis after burying over 129 Jews who were executed by the SS during the liquidation of the Zawiercie ghetto. The Nazis forced Srulik and Herschel to collect and bury the dead bodies scattered through the ghetto and then killed the two of them. Srulik and Herschel were the only members from either of our families who had a known grave. We went with a group of fellow survivors from our Fraternal Order of Bendin-Sosnowicer Sick and Benevolent Society (one of the last remaining "Landsmanshaftn" in New York City). We said kaddish together and then toured our hometowns and shared our stories.

I went back by myself one more time with a group of women who had been with me at Grünberg. We retraced the Death March route from my forced labor camp to Flossenbürg concentration camp where they were finally liberated in April 1945. A wonderful man, Mr. Robinson, organized the trip and made all the arrangements. He was an American soldier who had married a girl who had been with me in Grünberg, Amalie Mary Reichmann Robinson.

Srodula Ghetto, Sosnowiec 1988

My daughter-in-law Sara and me at my home at Targowa 21, Sosnowiec 1988

Henry in front of his house on our first return trip with Melvin, Sara and me, Siewierz 1988

Henry's grandfather Leibisch Rosenblatt's house, Siewierz 1988. This is where his father Mordechai Menachem and his Uncle Chil lived as children

Henry's brother Yankel's house in the back of Henry's house, Siewierz 1988

What Henry's house looked like, Siewierz 1997

Henry and me sharing pictures with former neighbors who are sitting where the synagogue once stood, Siewierz 1997. Only three Jews survived from the town

Henry and me with the neighbor who let Henry's father put on tefillin and pray in her home every morning because her house had no windows, Siewierz 1997

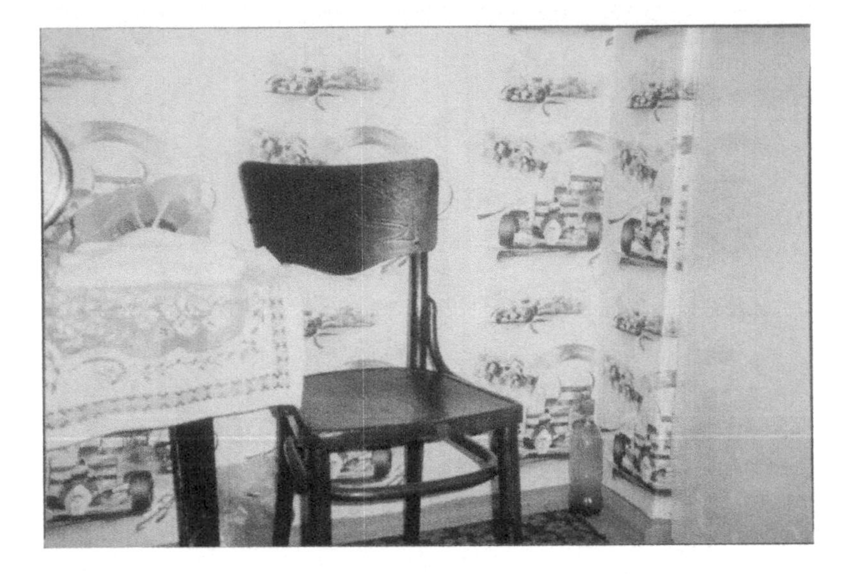

Chair that Henry's father used every morning for prayers, saved by the neighbor for fifty years, Siewierz 1997

Henry sitting on his father's chair in neighbor's house, Siewierz 1997

Henry and me in the courtyard of my home at Targowa 21, Sosnowiec 1997

My home at Targowa 21, Sosnowiec 1999

Me at The Dulag - former Skladowa Jewish Girls' Business School, Sosnowiec 1997

Me inside my old barracks with the skylight at Grünberg, 1997

The farm/estate, Shloss Gut, Streidelsdorf, Poland where I worked and hid after escaping from the Death March 1945, 1997

Schloss Gut, the farm/estate before the war, Streidelsdorf, Poland

Me at the Dulag Memorial plaque, Sosnowiec 1999

Henry at the memorial plaque for his brothers, Srulik and Herschel in Zawiercie Cemetery, 1999

Me at Helena’s grave in Furth, Germany, 1997

# CHAPTER 14

# THE GOOD LIFE

## Vacations, Trips, and Visitors

Henry and I loved to travel and as it became easier and more affordable, we took many trips to Israel and Europe. We always tried to stop by Helena's grave in Germany. We toured Italy, Spain, and France; another time we went to Scandinavia. We made several trips to health spas in Czechoslovakia. We went to Rio de Janeiro, Caracas, and the Caribbean islands.

We loved being in Israel and went many times, especially when Lillian lived there. These were not relaxing trips. Lillian took us on adventurous trips all over Israel and we ran around visiting all our relatives and friends. One year, the whole family spent Passover together in Israel for the bar mitzvah of my grandson Jonathan/Nati, who was named for my brother Natan. Melvin arranged several exciting family tours during the bar mitzvah trip and I went on all of them, including a hiking trip in Tel Dan nature reserve, jumping over rocks in streams and going through bushes.

Back in Brooklyn, our apartment was always filled with people traveling to America. Relatives from all over the world would visit and stay for long periods of time. It was a great opportunity to be close to the remnants of our family. Our Israeli cousins stayed with us for months after they finished their military service. Simon from Australia came every other year for business and sometimes brought his family. His son also lived with us when he moved to America.

In the winters, we went to the Saxony Hotel in Miami Beach. It was luxurious to stay in a hotel and eat in a fancy dining room and have everything taken care of for you. We had so many friends around and we were busy day and night. In the later years, we went to Desert Hot Springs, near Palm Springs, with other survivors. The climate was better for my arthritis. We stayed in efficiencies with a pool and traveled to Las Vegas and Los Angeles from there. It wasn't as fancy or as much fun as Miami Beach, but we still had good times

In the summers, we enjoyed going to the bungalow colonies in the Catskills. We bought a summer cottage in Sackett Lake near Monticello where Belinda had many friends. It was a small community based around a shul, and everyone was very friendly—it became our new family of friends. Each family member became a personal friend, no matter their age. In a way, the Sackett Lake community replaced the "Continentals." Belinda and Jack bought a house there as well and Sackett Lake became a place where the whole family gathered in the summer and for the High Holidays.

For our fiftieth wedding anniversary, our children gave us a gift of a cruise/land trip to Alaska and it was fantastic.

## Holidays

Our family was very close and the entire family spent most Jewish holidays together. As we got older, each of my children hosted a different holiday. Lillian always had a Hanukkah holiday party and I used to stand in her kitchen, frying hundreds of potato latkes. Melvin had a very large sukkah that could fit all of us and we often went to him. We all went to Sackett Lake for

Rosh Hashanah and stayed at Belinda's house. The shul in Sackett Lake had become a major part of our lives. Rabbi Breyer and Rabbi Lamm were more than our rabbinic leaders, they were our personal friends. We knew every single member and it was like davening with a large extended family. Henry loved davening there and everyone waited for his loud and heartfelt "duchening" Priestly Blessing as well as my son-in-law Jack's shofar blowing.

In 1991, we began a wonderful family tradition of taking the whole family to a hotel for Passover. It was one of the best things Henry and I ever did and everyone looked forward to Passover all year long. For many years, we went to the Saxony Hotel and had the most special times there with our children and grandchildren. The hotel had seen better days but our family loved everything about the place—the maître d', the waiters, the pool guy, the shuffleboard court, the solarium where we had our seders, and the guests who came every year and became our extended Pesach family. Our grandchildren have lifelong memories from those times that they always talk about. We continued our family tradition at the Majestic Hotel in Fort Lauderdale after the Saxony Hotel closed.

Henry viewed Passover as our personal holiday where we could celebrate our freedom from slavery. We had beautiful private seders and everyone participated in reading and discussing the Haggadah. Our seders were long and fun. We talked and sang a lot. Many years, other family members or close friends joined us and our seders grew to thirty people. I always made my special charoset to bring to the seder, and some years we even brought our own raw horseradish so we could watch Henry turn purple as he ate the bitter herb. Henry always liked to end by having us all dance in a circle, singing "L'Shana Haba B'Yerushalim," Next Year in Jerusalem.

Lillian, Belinda, and Melvin were always with us for Pesach but in later years it was sometimes difficult for the grandchildren to come because of their school schedules or other obligations. Nonetheless, we have kept this tradition, and last year, in 2019, almost 95 percent of the family, including the grandchildren and great-grandchildren, were there. I was looking forward to going again this year in 2020, even at my advanced age of ninety-seven, but unfortunately all the Passover programs were canceled because of the coronavirus.

We were proud and thankful to be Americans and always celebrated Thanksgiving with a huge dinner that included family, in-laws, friends, and anyone who didn't have a Thanksgiving meal to go to. Sometimes we needed three turkeys! Belinda and Melvin took turns hosting and it was a real feast, with everyone bringing their special side dishes and desserts. I always brought my apple cake. It also became a time where we celebrated my second birthday of the year, together with my grandson Zev.

Henry and I loved America and appreciated all the opportunities that the country had given us. We became citizens on November 9, 1956, and voted in every single election since then. I even voted in the last presidential election of 2016. We never took the freedom and security that we felt as Americans for granted.

That sense of security was destroyed in the 9/11 attacks on the World Trade Center in 2001. It was shocking that America had been attacked and I was terrified. All my horrible wartime memories came rushing back; I felt like it was 1939 and another world war was starting. It was a very frightening time.

On that beautiful morning, I was waiting for Henry on Forty-seventh Street and he was very late. It was obvious from the way people were acting that something bad had happened, but nobody knew exactly what. Henry finally arrived and told me he had been on the subway and saw the Twin Towers burning. Everything in the city was standing still and there was no way to get back to Brooklyn. We decided to walk to Lillian's; she lived on the Upper West Side. I went over to a packed bus stopped at a red light and begged the driver to take us; he opened the door and we stood on the steps inside the bus up Sixth Avenue. My son-in-law Jeff was in the area when the towers were hit and he was in total shock. We squeezed into their small apartment along with Jeff's father, Bill, and watched the news over and over again. The world felt like it was falling apart and I never thought that I would have to feel that fear again.

## The Next Generation

I loved being a bubbe and was very close with all my grandchildren. Each of my eight grandchildren was my most special treasure and my best revenge against the Nazis. I babysat all the time and the grandchildren slept over at my house in Brooklyn and Sackett Lake. I played cards, games, and ball, picked berries, and had fun times like I did with my kids. I even once broke my toe playing soccer with Belinda's boys. I loved cooking and baking for my grandchildren and they loved to come to my house and have my vegetable soup, sugar cookies in my special tin box, and, of course, my apple pie. Henry and I were so close with our grandchildren that sometimes we treated them just like our children and were too strict with them! My great-grandchildren call me "Big Bubbe."

Henry and I were fortunate to have a special part in all of our grandchildren's bar and bat mitzvahs. We kvelled with pride and were so happy to sit in the center of the circle while everyone danced around us. We tried so hard to keep everyone connected to G-d and religion and each of our grandchildren, in their own way, showed us that they understood the importance of our message.

Thank G-d the family has continued to grow and be successful. Five of my eight grandchildren are now married to wonderful people, and I have four great-grandchildren so far. I have three more grandsons to marry off and, with G-d's help, I plan to be at each of their weddings, celebrating and dancing with them.

Belinda's sons are all married: Ruvin married Erika Schneider, his high school sweetheart, and they have two boys, Sam and Judah, and a little girl, Sarina, and they live in Brooklyn. Zev married Jenny Gill from Riverdale and they live in Portland, Oregon; and Abe married Catherine Eyre-Walker from Melbourne and they live in Sydney, Australia. Two of Melvin's children are married: Danielle married Daniel Mendelsohn, a British young man, and they have a little girl, Kira. They met in Israel and lived there before recently moving to New Rochelle, New York. Jonathan married his high school sweetheart, Ahuva Zucker from Brooklyn, and they live in Riverdale, New

York. Melvin's youngest son, Matthew, is in college, as is Lillian's youngest son, Daniel. Lillian's oldest son, Gabriel, lives in Manhattan and is an architect. I am proud of all my grandchildren. They are hard workers and are successful in their careers and lives.

Henry and I were independent for a long time. One of the hardest things for both of us was when he had to give up driving. The kids asked him on his ninetieth birthday, "You've seen so many changes in your life. What was the one that made the biggest difference to you in your lifetime?" He answered without a moment of hesitation—driving. For Henry, it was driving and owning his own car. After Henry gave up driving, we used Access-A-Ride to get into the city and do shopping and errands. At a certain point, we began to accept the fact that we needed aides in the house.

We had a wonderful life in Brooklyn—we were part of a lively Jewish community; we had our children and grandchildren, cousins and other relatives and our many friends. We were busy all the time. We went to so many affairs—weddings, sheva brachas, bar mitzvahs—we were busy every week. Those years were glorious and filled with so many happy events.

## CHAPTER 15

# GETTING OLDER AND NEW CHALLENGES

### Health

I have lived my whole life in physical pain. I never fully recovered from the starvation and suffering I experienced during the Holocaust. I was often hospitalized and had several serious operations. I had a bad back, intestinal problems, ulcers, arthritis, and horrible migraines. Later I developed rheumatoid arthritis and osteoporosis. I was once tall, five foot seven, and now I am probably only five feet because I am so bent over.

In 1971, I was hospitalized for four months with complications from a blockage in my small intestine, often in critical condition. This was a very long time to be in the hospital with two kids still at home. My husband was stuck managing everything but never complained

In 1989, I was diagnosed with possible liver cancer. The doctor told me to get my affairs in order as I only had a few months to live. It was a terrible shock for the family. Then a true miracle happened. The machine needed to do my liver biopsy broke down and my doctor, Dr. Slattery decided to retake the CAT scan while we waited for the machine to be fixed. This saved my life because the scan showed the mass to be a birthmark and not cancerous. If they had done the liver biopsy, I would have bled to death. Henry and Melvin believed that G-d had intervened and saved my life.

In 2006, I had another medical miracle when my son saved my life. I was rushed to the hospital in horrible pain. Melvin came to check on me while I was still in the emergency room. As he walked in, he saw that my vital signs were crashing and I was near death. Melvin took charge, managed the medical emergency, and saved my life while the other doctors watched in respect. It turned out I had sepsis from a blockage in my gallbladder. The other doctors weren't even aware of how critical the situation had become and stepped back to let Melvin handle my care. Melvin miraculously arrived just in time to save my life.

Yet, I always lived life to the fullest as much as I could, even when I was in pain. Despite all my many and various physical conditions, my mind remains sharp. My memory is incredible. I remember so many details. Sometimes I am not sure if it is a curse or a blessing.

## Losing Henry

Henry was the healthy one and I was the sick one. He was so strong—like a bull, even in his early nineties. He suffered from bad knees and stenosis, which forced him to use a walker and then a wheelchair in his last year of life. He began to fade physically in his last months but his mind remained sharp until his last few days. He was determined to keep managing his affairs until the end and wrote checks for his February bills and arranged doctor appointments. He knew his time was coming to an end and he was trying to prepare himself. The Shabbos before he died, he told me he saw his parents and brothers dancing on our bedroom ceiling, waiting for him.

We took him to the hospital that Sunday for hydration and his condition worsened quickly. My last moments with Henry were as romantic as our lives together. He gave me a Valentine's Day kiss from his hospital bed and told me he would be home with me soon. We had always celebrated Valentine's

Day since our days in Springfield, even though it was a Christian holiday. Later that night, he lost consciousness. Henry died at 9:30 a.m. on Thursday morning, February 16, 2017, at ninety-six years old. I was so sure he was going to live to one hundred.

I wasn't with Henry when he died and I have never been able to forgive myself for not being next to him when he needed me the most. My children had sent me home to rest because they were worried about my health. It was cruel to lose Henry. We were married for seventy-one years and he had been the love of my life for over seventy-five years. We understood each other better than anyone in the world and were lucky to have had a long and happy life together. I miss him so much every day.

## Henry's Unveiling and My Last Trip to Israel

Henry was buried in Israel in Har HaMenuchot overlooking Jerusalem in a family plot he had carefully chosen many years earlier. That June, Lillian, Belinda, Melvin, Sara and I went to Israel to put up his matzeva/gravestone. Henry had spent a lot of time planning the matzeva and our children followed his instructions. The names of our parents and siblings were inscribed on a memorial stone that was placed between our double plot. In this way, we honored all of our loved ones who had no grave of their own. The unveiling was filled with our Israeli relatives and friends and other visitors to Israel. Everyone spoke beautifully about Henry and his legacy.

It was like a knife stabbing my heart to see Henry's name, Chil HaKohen Rosenblatt, engraved on the matzeva. It was made doubly hard by seeing the stone with the list of all our dead loved ones. It wasn't only Henry that I was mourning but all of those I had loved and lost. I was lost in my painful memories and my grief was overwhelming.

It was a very sad trip but I knew I was lucky to have children who wanted to be with me and were willing to do everything they could for me. They refused to let me sit and grieve and schlepped me around in a wheelchair—it was the only time I permitted myself to go in a wheelchair—to the Kotel, the Old and New City of Jerusalem, and Tel Aviv–Jaffa. When it was time to leave Israel, I was beside myself. I knew I would never see Henry's matzeva again in my lifetime. I wondered how I would be able to go on with my life. I cried the whole plane ride home.

## Being a Widow

It was difficult for me to figure out how to live alone. I knew from all my losses that you have to be patient because time helps heal the pain. Fortunately, that September, I was asked to participate in the Witness Theater program at the Yeshivah of Flatbush. I went every week all year long, with seven other Holocaust survivors, and sat with a group of students as they asked questions about my life. They listened to me so intently as I shared my experiences about the Holocaust and my life that I realized that I did have a reason to live. I needed to share my story with as many young people for as long as I could. Witness Theater gave me the strength to go on.

At the end of the school year, Witness Theater puts on a performance written and acted by the survivors and students. We performed at Yeshivah of Flatbush, a local public high school, Kingsborough College, and finally the Museum of Jewish Heritage. My message for Witness Theater was, "Being a fighter means never giving up and standing up for what's right and true."

The students became my new friends. They are the most wonderful kids and I love them all, especially Jacqueline, who acted as me in our performance. She has become like my adopted daughter. Members of my Witness Theater group have continued to call and visit me and bring their families along to hear my story. We talked about their families, their problems, and their future goals as well as my life. The yeshivah has continued to invite me to school events and seminars to teach new students.

I have participated in other school programs, including Names, Not Numbers, once for Magen David Yeshivah and then for a mixed group of schools in Queens and Long Island—HAFTR (Hebrew Academy of the Five Towns and Rockaway), BELL Academy Middle School, and a public school. I go wherever I am invited to share my story. In the past, Henry used to do most of the talking when we spoke to groups but now it is up to me. I can't believe that I had the courage to get on the stage for so many strangers at the Museum of Jewish Heritage but I did it.

I started to go to luncheons and special programs in my neighborhood that were organized specifically for Holocaust survivors. Selfhelp, Blue Card, and other organizations had programs matching volunteers and Holocaust survivors and I have met the nicest people through these programs.

I am very close with my children and I am part of their everyday lives. Their friends have been my friends and they are part of my family. I have been invited to all their simchas and we have remained close as we all got older. Our families have celebrated Passover, Rosh Hashanah, and Thanksgiving together for many years. Some of these friends are the children of my good friends who are no longer alive. Our legacy of friendships are being carried on by the next generation as their children also call and visit me. I love hearing from the young people and appreciate that they want to be part of my life.

I am lucky because I have always loved people and they have loved me in return. So many people have reached out to me, visited, and called to keep me company and hear my story. It is people who have given me the strength to continue and it is their love that keeps me filled with the joy of living despite suffering even a greater loss since Henry's death.

## More Heartache—a Devastating Loss

Last Yom Kippur, in 2019, something unimaginable happened—my son, my baby, Melvin, died from a rare and deadly cancer. The pain and shock of his death have been unbearable. He was a wonderful son, always attending to my every need. Melvin had always been my pride and joy, and from an early age, he had been my protector. He tried to protect me to the very end, never letting me know how sick he was. I will never understand why G-d did not take me, an old lady who has lived a long life, and save the life of my young, brilliant son who spent his whole life doing good as a dedicated doctor. He should have been rewarded with a long, happy life.

I have suffered great tragedy in my life and somehow kept going. I lost my oldest daughter and my youngest son, and the pain is indescribable. I have mourned for the life that Helena never had a chance to live and I don't believe I will ever understand why my baby, my only son, the one with golden hands and heart, was taken so suddenly and unfairly. It has been so bitter to bear the tragedy of Melvin's death all alone without my beloved Henry's support.

It's a tough life. I thought I had lived through everything imaginable, but G-d wasn't done yet. The coronavirus struck in a year where I need to be with people more than ever, and instead I have been totally isolated. I miss people and I miss my routine. The pandemic is a terrible thing but I know it will end, and in the meantime, I am healthy, safe, well-fed, and can speak to my loved ones at any time. These are not the terrible days of the Holocaust. My message is to be patient and strong—better days are coming.

## Continued Life

I don't know how I have had the strength to keep going day after day. Even I am amazed at how strong I am. What am I made of? Who could bear all this and keep going? I have no answers—I only know to be a fighter and stay strong. I learned two important values in life at a young age: respect your parents, especially your mother, and never stop fighting for what you want and what you believe.

I have lived a long life and am fortunate to remember so much in vivid detail. These memories have helped me find the strength to survive and live a wonderful, rich life. It is in G-d's hands how my story will end, but I have to keep doing the things I know—fight to my last dying breath and love the people and world around me as much as I can.

Many years ago, Henry told a reporter the following: "If all the oceans and rivers were ink and every person in the world a writer, the story of Nazi Germany could never still be written. . . . I found myself questioning G-d and asking, Why, Why? But in the end, it was faith that carried us through."

I have tried in Henry's honor and in honor of our families and loved ones who we lost to write our story for my children, my grandchildren, my great-grandchildren. I am very proud of all of you. I trust that this book will let my memories live on forever.

To my family and friends, both young and old, I say to each and every one of you, "Good luck and I wish you a beautiful future."

My grandson Jonathan and Ahuva's wedding, March 2017.
Sara, me, Jonathan and Melvin

Henry's Unveiling at Har HaMenuchot, Israel, June 2017. L to R: cousins, Tal, Kobi Lefkowitz' daughter; Hana and Moshe Lavy; Chana Rosenblatt; Danielle; me; Lillian; Belinda; friends, Daniel Tauber, Judy Ziedenweber; Danielle's husband, Daniel Mendelsohn

Lillian, me, Melvin, Belinda at Kotel/Wailing Wall, June 2017

Henry's First Yahrzeit, February 2017. L to R: First Row – Ruvin; Sammy; Erika; Zev; Judah; Lillian; Jack. Second Row – Abe; me; Jeff; Belinda; Jonathan; Melvin

Me with my great granddaughter Sarina, April 2018

My grandson Zev and Jenny's wedding, 2018. L to R: Me; Jenny; Zev; Ruvin; Jack; Abe; Catherine; Belinda; Erika holding Sarina; Sam; Judah

Me with my grandson Zev at his wedding, June 2018

Me, Melvin, Danielle and my great granddaughter Kira, Passover 2019

Melvin, Jonathan, Ahuva, Sara, Danielle, Kira, and Daniel, Passover 2019

My great granddaughter Kira's first birthday party.
Me with Melvin, Gabe and Danny standing, June 2019

Me and Belinda, Ruvin, Erika and my great grandchildren, Sam, Judah and Sarina, Seminar February 2020

Cousin Simon's family visiting from Australia. Belinda, Simon's daughter Marilyn, his granddaughters Talia and Stephanie, and me, May 2019

Me with Jacqueline who played "Mira" at Witness Theater Performance, 2018

Me and my grandson Matthew, Sara and her father David Einhorn at a Holocaust Survivors' Luncheon, January 2020

My weekly visit with Yeshivah of Flatbush students, March 2, 2020

My grandson Abe and Catherine's wedding, March 2019. L to R: Danny, Sara, Melvin, Jeff, Lillian, me, Belinda, Abe, Catherine, Jack, Jenny, Zev, Erika, Ruvin, Jonathan, Ahuva and Judah, Sammy and Sarina

Me, Lillian and Belinda, March 2019

Post Rosh HaShanah, September 2020. L to R: Standing, Jeff, Lillian, Ruvin and Erika. Seated, Jack, me and Belinda

Me with Melvin, my fixer, 2018

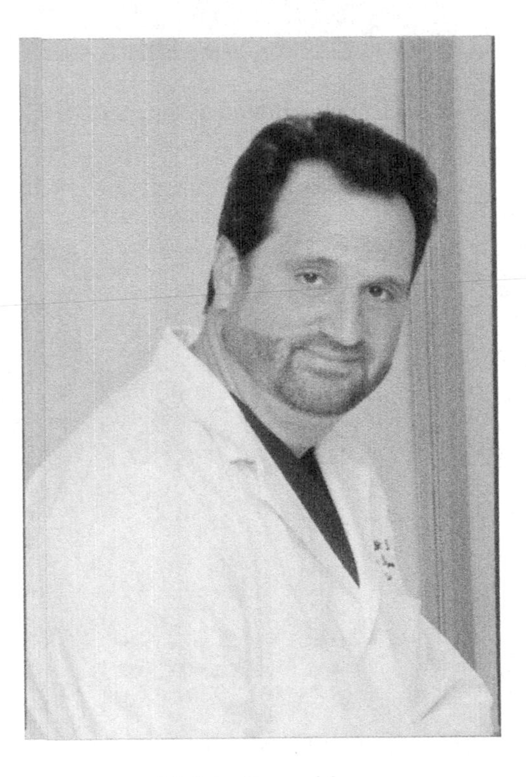

Melvin Rosenblatt
December 21, 1958 – October 8, 2019

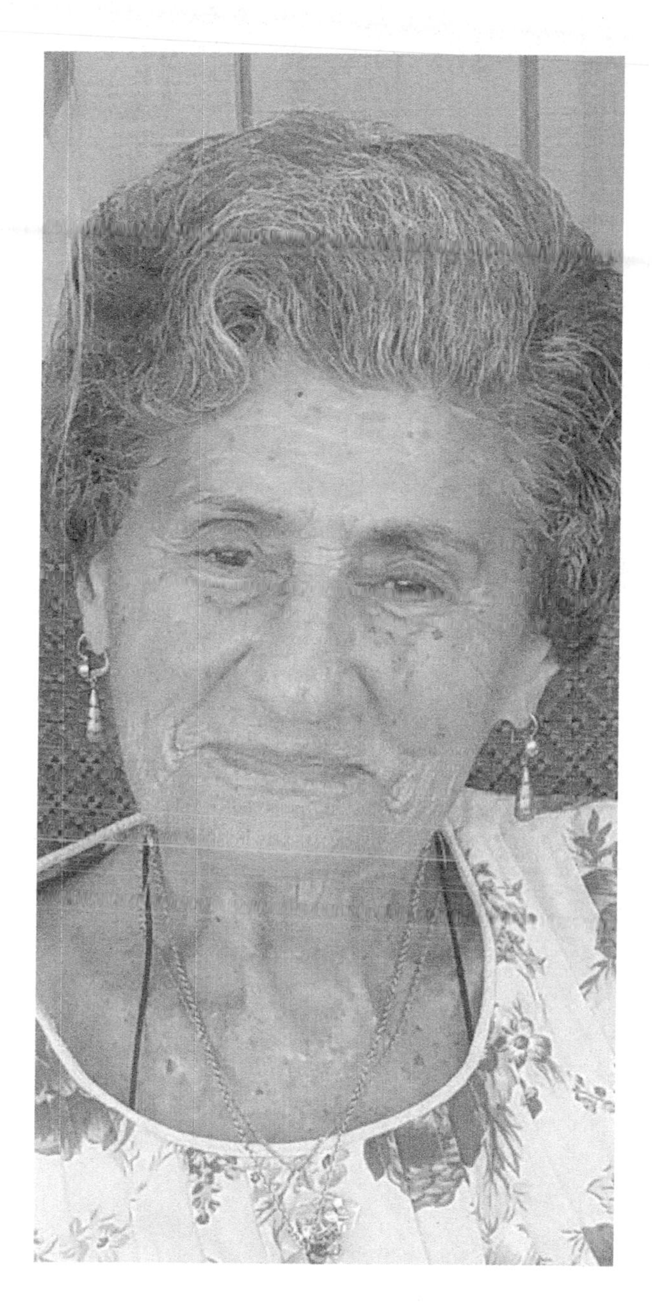

Me, August 2019

# PART III:

# HENRY ROSENBLATT: HOLOCAUST SURVIVOR IN HIS WORDS

# MY NAME IS HENRY ROSENBLATT: FIRST DAYS OF THE WAR

*[written on twenty-five pieces of scrap paper in the 1990s]*

My name is Henry Rosenblatt. In Germany they called me Heinrich. In Poland they called me Henriek. In Yiddish, my name is Yehiel HaKohen, the son of Mendel, or in Hebrew, Mordechai Menachem HaKohen. My mother was Chaya—her maiden name was also Rosenblatt from Bełchatów, Poland, which was not far from Lodz. She was a relative—all the Rosenblatts that are Kohanim are relatives in Poland—and they were very *frum* or religious people. They married in the family because they knew the family; they wanted to make shitachs that are not *psulim* (damaged). This way the family knew that everything is okay.

I was born in Poland in a small shtetl, the name was Siewierz, not far from Będzin and Zawiercie. The date of my birth is August 2, 1919. I was the youngest of my brothers. I was the sixth child. I also had a sister who was two years younger than I. Together there were seven children—six brothers and one sister. After the war, I am the only one from my family that survived the Holocaust.

The names of my brothers were: the oldest brother was Jankil (Yankel), he was married before the war to a girl from Zduńska Wola near Lodz. Her name was Hindela or Hinda, her maiden name Rosenblatt, and she was also related. They had three or four children. I don't remember the names. [33] I think they were all boys and they lived in Siewierz in the back of our house. The house, the one house I remember, I was a kid when my father built this house for them in our yard and then they got married. My second brother, his name was Wolf, they called him Welvel. He was also married before the war. He married a girl from Zawiercie. Her maiden name was Haberman, but I do not remember her first name. They also had three or four children, and he was living in Zawiercie on Govno Schloska Street. He had a store selling candy and cigarettes and a gasoline station. The third brother, his name was Abraham, they called him Abrovela. He was married to a girl from Pabianice. Her maiden name was Kalınstam, her father was a "*morenu,*" a very learned man, like a rabbi. He *paskened schales* (ruled on difficult religious questions). It was a very nice family—the father became very rich in Pabianice. He had a factory from textiles and a wholesale business from candy and cigarettes. Abraham had two children, I do not remember any more if they were boys or girls. The fourth brother, his name was Israel, they called him Srulik. He was not married. Srulik had a good business, he had lumber yards in Myszków and also in Upper Silesia near Bytom. The fifth brother, his name was Herschel. He was not married; he worked in the store with my father. My father had a grocery store with general merchandise. I was away most of the time, away sitting and learning in yeshivas. I had a sister. Her name was Surela; she was the youngest and she was such a young girl. We were a very happy family.

*[Henry's mother died when he was ten or eleven years old; his father sent him to yeshivas in other towns where he boarded with strangers.]*

[33] Dan Burns's 2004 document with Yankel and Hindela's four children's names and birthdates: Josef April 3, 1927; Chaja May 6, 1929; Rywka December 17, 1930; and Chaskiel Lajb April 20, 1939.

I still remember my youth when I was home. I came home for holidays from the yeshiva. I was very *frum* (religious). My friends used to be jealous of me that I learned very well. I had good Rebbes in yeshivas and I became a big Talmud "*chuchem*" (learned person). I used to stay up all night learning. I was an organizer and organized a trip from the yeshiva to big rabbis' graves shortly before the war. This was in 1938 when Poland made a mobilization and they called up all the boys who were able to pay to get out of being drafted for the army earlier. In our house my father did everything possible that the boys, his sons, should not go to the Polish army because of problems with Shabbos and kosher food. But that was before the fear of war; during this time, nothing could be done to get free—no money in the world was enough. Then I had to come home to help my father in the business.

When the war broke out, my two brothers were in the army, Srulik and Herschel. I was home with my father and sister and stepmother. I worked hard in the business. I worked up a good business, we had a lot of customers. I always brought fresh goods so business was very good before the war, even the Pollakim [Polish people] came, even with the boycott when they were told not to buy from Jewish merchants. But we had the goods that the Poles didn't have, so even then things were very good. We knew that a war would break out. We did not know how soon, maybe not, and then the Polish army said that they were strong so not to worry. We did not have a place we could run away to because all the doors for the Polish Jewish people were closed. Nobody wanted to let us in. We got stuck in Poland.

FRIDAY MORNING, September 1, 1939, 5:00 a.m., I saw planes flying over our town. In the beginning we thought that it was Polish planes. The propaganda was that England would help Poland and then I thought it was English planes, but soon we found out that it was German planes and the war would start soon. We found out that Germans were arriving in Poland, that the Polish army was running away, that it was very bad. Our town was very close to the German border. What were we to do? Where should we run? We had the store open all day. Friday was very busy, people bought everything; we ran out of merchandise. We had in the basement extra merchandise and groceries. Shabbos was Shabbos—we closed the store and went to shul. All day on Shabbos, we saw Polish soldiers running away, leaving the people *hefker* (in chaos). I think this was the first Selichos (prayers said before the Rosh Hashanah) night. We went to say Selichos on Saturday night, and afterward we all started to run away with wagons and horses, by foot, to run away from the Germans, but German planes came and started bombing on the people. There were thousands and thousands of people on the road, old, young children, and babies. We walked all day. Sunday my father, my sister, my brother Yankel and his wife and the small children were all on foot and the weather was very hot. All of a sudden, we saw Germans fly past on motorcycles, but they did not do anything to us. Here I decided to go back home because we did not have a place to run away from them because they [the Germans] were faster. They were coming with tanks and we were walking on foot. But my father and stepmother, and sister and brother Yankel with Hindela his wife and small children—we all wanted Father to stop in Zawiercie because the Germans already came in.

I had a married brother, Wolf, living in Zawiercie with small children. There my father and the other brother Yankel with his wife and children and my stepmother all remained. I came back home to Siewierz that Sunday night because we had a business and lots of groceries and general merchandise. My first cousin came with me; his name was Mordechai but they called him Modek Wajcman. He stayed with me in my house. In Europe the business was together with your house where you lived. We went to sleep Sunday night, that was September 3—the third day since the war started. In the middle of the night, something woke me and we saw people were trying to break into the store. They were ready to go in and to rob the store but my cousin and I started to make a lot of noise and they ran away. Monday morning, we got up very early and we opened the *ladens* (shutters). In Europe you used to have *ladens* on the outside of the house and then you closed the windows for the night. When you opened the *laden* you could look out. When I looked out, I saw a lot of soldiers marching in the road. I was young and did not know if this was German or English or French. They told us that the British/French would come to help the Polish. We closed the *ladens* back up because we were afraid. About 10:00 a.m. my cousin went out to find out what was going on. One hour later Mordechai came back and told me that these soldiers were German and they already killed a lot of people. On the road were kids watching the soldiers' marching. My cousin also told me that they put on the walls from the buildings proclamations that the Germans took over the town and all the people should go back to work and all the stores should open. Those who will not obey the rules will be shot.

I did not know what to do—to open the store or not. Later in the day I opened the store and soldiers came in the store to buy bread, cigarettes, chocolate, etc., and they paid with German marks and I really did not know the value of the mark. After two hours, I closed the store; it got dark at night. I was thinking what to do—I took a lot of groceries and put them in the cellar. I did not want to sell everything. Tuesday morning, I was afraid, but I opened the store again. Only German soldiers came in to buy and I was alone at home with my cousin. I stood behind the counter and the Germans bought everything. The store was filled with the soldiers. Tuesday afternoon my oldest brother, Yankel, with his wife and children came back and my brother came to help me in the store.

Late in the afternoon when we stood at the counter serving to the German soldiers, five SA soldiers—special brown uniforms—[came in] and asked me and my brother and my cousin if we were Juden. [34] We said yes—and they said, "Sie sensenalle Verhaftel" (you are detained). They took us out from the store and onto the street, put us against the wall, and said we were *alla Ershon*, that we will all be killed. We stood with our hands high. In the meantime, the store *gefallen hefker* (fell into disarray) and the soldiers took everything from the store. They did not let us take anything and we stayed against the wall with our hands high and the street filled with people. Then the SA took us away to the public school/church—one was next to the other—with no food, no water, and it was still very hot. We were in the school for two days. In the meantime, my brother's wife, Hindela, found out where we were. She came over and brought us water and bread to eat. Nobody knew what to do with us. It was not only Jews; there were Polish people also there. After two

---

[34] SA were Special Forces—Sturmabeilung, literally, Storm Detachment—of the Nazi Party paramilitary organization.

days of being in the school, it was already Thursday, they took me out with ten other people. We did not know where we were going, but later they took us into the forest to be with people who had been with us at the school on the first day.

Later the soldiers they took us to the big church in town and they started to let most of the Polish people go and the Jews they kept. The next day, on Friday, they brought big army trucks and they put us on the truck and took us to Czestochowa into barracks. The Polish soldiers were already there because they all went to war. They put us in the barracks together with the Polish people and held us there for some days. After then they took us out from the barracks and put us in a big yard. The military came into the big yard and put out straw and told us to run and to pick up this straw. In the meantime, they brought a lot of Jews that they caught on the road from Lodz, etc., and from all the towns around Lodz, Zduńska Wola. Big rabbis were part of the group. We had to run like that for two hours and they hit us with the rifles to run faster. A lot of the people died from this running. After we finished running, they did not let me go back to the same barracks where I was together with Polish people. Now we were in different barracks, only for Jews. They told us to run to the barracks. They put extra wood in our way before we ran back to the barrack and the people stepped over this and fell down one after the other and they began to hit the people with their rifles—faster, faster, *schnell, schnell.* After we got into this barrack, they put big boards in front of the door and gave an order: leave everything that we had with us in the barrack and if we did not do this, they would do a complete check on each person. If they did find something by him—money or gold or watches or knives—the person would be shot on the spot. Naturally all the people were afraid, and they put everything in this barrack—gold, money, watches, rings. Everything we had we put in. I put in my watches and some gold pieces and money but I left by me some money because I said without any money, I am dead already.

After they finished collecting all the money and the jewelry, they closed the doors of the barracks. The barracks were full of people; there was not a place for anybody to stand. A lot of us pulled ourselves up by the beams from the barracks to hold on. It was very hot. I think this was the night of Rosh Hashanah. In the middle of the night it started to rain. We were knocking on the doors that they should open the doors. Finally, they opened the doors so that we could have a little air and they called out ten people and gave us empty bottles to go for water. I brought a bottle; Yankel was with me. I give him a little water just to make the lips good and wet and the rest I took and sprayed it on the people so everybody would have just a little bit of water to make their lips wet. People stood by the door and took some of the rainwater dripping from the roof and so went the night of Rosh Hashanah. The next day we were in the barrack and they let us be outside, but no food no water. No one had a siddur. We davened; it was the second day of Rosh Hashanah and then came an order to ship us out to Germany.

Late in the day they took us to the trains and there were a lot of freight trains standing on the track. The soldiers ordered us in this train very quickly and they hit us with their rifles to go faster into this train. The freight train had no steps and you had to jump to go in. Not everybody could do this and some got hurt very badly and were bleeding. We were traveling in this train in the day and one night and the next day we arrived in Germany and to a place outside Görlitz, which was a big city. They took us into the open and it was raining very hard and we got very cold. We did not have any shoes because they took away the shoes from us, so were walking barefoot. The guards were watching. We warmed each other, we were very wet from the rain, we could not lie down. The ground was all mud so we stood in a circle to warm each other.

In the middle of the night, one SA man or special SS soldier came into the tent and they said they needed ten men to bring food for the two hundred and fifty men who were in this tent. I volunteered for this and they give us ten big pots and every head got a cup. We went to bring from the kitchen soup for the two hundred and fifty people in our tent, but the ground was very wet and slimy and muddy. When we stepped in this mud with our feet, we could not take them out so fast. So by the time we came back to the tent, all the soup got spilled out—and all the people who were waiting for this soup—there was nothing left in the pot to give them. We went hungry and wet; we were standing all night in this tent.

In the morning an older officer came and he said that we would get bread and marmalade or jam on the bread and would get back to the train and travel farther into Germany. We had a piece of bread and a little bit of jam and after that we walked to the train wagons. We went into this wagon and the train started moving. We looked out through the only little window and we saw German cities with stations. After two days of traveling we arrived in Luckenwalde, which was on the outskirts of Berlin. There were large tents standing with straw on the floor, so we could rest on the straw. The weather got a little bit better, so we walked around the courtyard under German watchmen, and we dried out a little bit. They organized a kitchen and we got soup and a piece of bread for most of the people. Many had already died, many from hunger. We buried them there in a Jewish cemetery and we were there until the day after Yom Kippur

We were fasting on Yom Kippur all day, but on that day we got bread and butter, but we did not eat in the morning. After Yom Kippur they told us we were going home. They took us back to the train, they give us bread, and we were on our way to go home. They kept us in the train for maybe ten days locked up in the cattle train. They did not let us out. Everything we needed to make, we made in the wagons. The smell and the stink were terrible. A lot of people died in the wagons.

Finally, after ten days they took us to Nuremberg and put us in the barrack where the guard soldiers were. We took out the dead people and we buried them in the Jewish cemetery. When we had to walk from the train to the barracks, we had to walk through the city. It was a sunny day and it was the last day of Sukkoth. The Jewish people tried to throw bread from the windows for us to catch, but the soldiers did not let us stop to pick it up. They started shooting at the windows from where the people threw the bread for us. Finally, we came to the barracks and we were there one week with food and water. We got water from the rain, and after the ten days again to the wagon trains, which brought us to Krakow, Poland. And they put us in a place they called Bomarkis [Banaken] outside of Krakow; it was a big flour factory and a mental hospital.

The Jewish committee brought us bread and the German guards were watching us after a vicious day. We heard that they made a deal with the Jewish committee. For money, they will let us out little by little every day. How would we pay the money for this person and that person to leave and who would be released? This was going on all week. What we did every day, they took us out from this place—about two hundred people—to the Jewish mikvah for a bath because we were full of lice and dirty. From this mikvah they took the people to a new place more suitable for the winter. Before the war in Poland, it was a crazy house (*Loszno*) for mental patients. When we were going from this Bomarkis [Banaken] house back onto the street, if the money was paid for an individual to be released, then the guards and the SS put them on the trolley at a big crossing in the street. They made us form two lines or three lines and the rest of us were marched to the new place in the crazy house.

I was with my brother Yankel and nobody knew where we were. The Jewish Gemeinde in Krakow got in touch with my family and a relative of ours came to Krakow with money. She was a young lady, she looked like a *shikse* (non-Jewish girl) because Jews were not allowed to travel away from home and they had to wear the Jewish Star of David. She arrived in Krakow on the last day of this operation. It was on a Friday morning. She came to the guards from the camp and paid the money to the SS or SA or to the soldiers. The soldiers called out our names in the camp and we came to the gate and saw this lady, our relative. She could not talk to us but the guards told us when we got back from the bathhouse that we should stay in the last line. In the meantime, when we went to the bathhouse, my relative arranged to throw in some clothing so we could change our clothes. This way, when the guards cut us off from marching in the line, the Polish people would not recognize that we were Jews from a camp. In the middle of the road, they cut me off with my brother Yankel from the line and the rest were marching further forward.

Jewish people were standing in the street and they grabbed us and took us to their house. We spent Shabbos with these people. These people were very nice; they made us a very nice Shabbos. Everything was so good because we were already two months without food and water and without washing. We were worse than the animals. We were in Krakow with these people over a week because we did not have any papers to travel until the Gemeinde helped us with papers.

We traveled home and it was winter already in Poland. My father was home, my brothers Herschel and Srulik came home from the Polish military. Thank Hashem we were together after so many months of separations, after so many people got killed. This was the winter of 1939–1940 and the Holocaust had just started. It was difficult to get food, and wood or coal for heat. Everything was rationed for the Jews, especially since we could no longer run to the Polish people or to the farm to buy something. It was very bad. My father, Ahuv HaShalom, was broken up; his beard and *payes* were hand-ripped-out by the Germans. My father covered his beard and *payes* with a scarf so as not to be as visible. The degradation was very big. All of the dignity was taken away from the Jews by the Germans. It was very bad, but we managed, handling it as long as we were together in the house.

We were out of range from the outside world, as newspapers and radio were not allowed. We did not know what was going on in the outside world. Sometimes we got some news from the Polish neighbors. We had to wear a Jewish star to be recognized as a Jews. Ladies wore stars in the front and in the back and men wore armbands with the star. If they caught you not wearing the star, they shot you on the spot because a Jew was restricted where he could move around. We could not go to the Polish people. We could not mix with the Polish people. We were separated from all the world. We could not travel from one town to the next town without a permit from the Germans. This was in 1940.

By the end of 1940, they started to take young people and ship them out to Germany in slave labor concentration camps. I was shipped out on November 11, 1940, to a slave labor camp in Auenrode, Germany. It was a very bad labor camp. It was winter. I was walking in a forest to cut trees and build railroad tracks. We worked about ten hours a day in the snow and it was very cold with little food, without warm clothes, without good shoes, only wooden shoes. A lot of people got sick and died. The only thing that kept you going was hope. You were hoping that tomorrow would be a better day and something would happen, somebody would come and help us, the Red Cross or somebody. But nobody came to help us, nobody wanted to help us. We were a totally forgotten people. We were no longer people, only numbers. We worked like this all winter, day in and day out, went to work, had Appells (roll calls) every day, and counted how many, day after day. I had a friend, a nurse in the Kranke S2 Building, and she was trying to help a group of boys get out. [35]

*[Writing ends abruptly.]*

## HENRY ROSENBLATT MEMOIRS TRANSLATED FROM YIDDISH

*[written in an old school notebook in early 1950s in Yiddish script—translated into English in 2017]*

[September 1939] The SS man in charge chased us with his hounds so we'd run faster, until we got to the munitions depot, and there we waited for a drop of soup, but the pot was empty. It had all spilled out on the way. And this is how we waited all night for a drop of soup. This is how the whole night passed—to stand in our socks and barefoot and dripping from the rain and cold all night.

We prayed with all our might for the dawn, for the sun to shine just a little bit. Finally, day dawned, and it was already Sunday, and this is how we stood out in the open, all day, trying to keep our heads up, with a little bowl in our hands, and waited for the coffee and bread because the soup had all run out.

It was Sunday before daylight and someone arrived ordering us to assemble in rows out in the open. They'd give us bread and marmalade, and they brought over to each column in this depot one-quarter kilo of bread and large vats of marmalade. And everyone approached and was given one-eighth

---

[35] Henry was released from Auenrode with the help of the nurse and returned to Poland in April 1941, shortly after Purim. It was at this time that he met Mira, his future wife.

of the army bread, half a tablespoon of marmalade for the bread, and a little coffee. And the foam of the coffee was a little sweet—we took a little comfort—and we were told this had to last until tomorrow, Monday night, because tomorrow morning they're removing us from here.

The whole night we waited for the morning, for them to lead us away at daybreak. So they told us to get up again and assemble and walk. They led us to the train yards. Everything had been prepared with freight wagons, and they loaded us into the wagons. And we traveled until arriving in Luckenwalde [near Berlin]. There we were unloaded again. High-ranking officers arrived, and long deliberations were held, and after that we had to fall into columns.

They started marching us all outside the city until they forced us into a certain camp, where they constructed hundreds and hundreds of these peculiar tents and primitive barracks. And there each of us was registered and everyone had a number hung around their neck and a large yellow

"Jude" Star of David on their breast.

And afterward they put us in the open tents, not in the constructed barracks. The constructed barracks were separated from our blocks with electric barbed wire. There they kept Polish prisoners of war. In the blocks where we were kept, they gave us straw to spread on the ground, and this is how we lay on the straw and slept on the straw. We were not handed any blankets. At night we were frozen from the cold. During the day, we stole a little warmth from the sun. We received food once a day, little turnips and a little boiled water. The turnips were hard as stone, and if someone wanted a little more and approached the kitchen, he was beaten back with a pole to the head.

We were guarded with electric barbed wire, and as an extra measure, every hut was guarded by two SS, one on one side of the hut, the second one, behind it.

We were unshaven and filthy from not having washed for such a long time, and no hair was cut, and from lying on the straw we were infested with giant lice. And the lice were feasting on us to their satiety. There were very many cases where the lice had massacred their victims, biting them to death, and the victims were buried there in Luckenwalde in the Jewish cemetery. They knew they could take people to bury from camp there and take their money.

They took out thirty young children and I was among them. And they were taken off to a large kettle with hot lime [lye]. And this is how they ordered us to stick our heads into the hot lime and our hair started to fall out. And to this very day my hair is still falling out. I spent an awful lot of money on my hair, various medicines, but it does no good. My hair keeps falling out. I used to have very lovely hair.

We were in Luckenwalde and suddenly an order arrives that we have to assemble in rows, and we were told they're sending us back home. And everyone was given half an army bread, and in my group a can of preserves, and we were told this had to last two days. As hungry as I was, I ate it up right away, even before they loaded us on the train. And they led us to the station and there were already three horse freight wagons prepared, enclosed with steel wires and sealed windows. And this is how we were shoved in like horses, with the door locked behind us. And a squadron of SS traveled along with us. And everyone was overjoyed that in two days we'd be back home.

In the meantime, two days passed, and we see and hear nothing, and also no food is handed out and every human need had to be done in the wagons and the stench was terrible. We were actually let out when the train stopped. And we begged to be let out for bodily needs, but it was senseless to do this, and we were not allowed, and the doors were locked with a lock, and SS guards were additionally provided.

After a few days traveling, we saw we had arrived on Polish soil, but we were not let out. After eight days we were let out along the paths like animals, not having eaten or drank, and every wagon was half full of corpses. This was how we traveled, with the corpses.

I remember how I had a cold infection from the frost and I was sure I wouldn't be able to breathe any longer. Our train suddenly stopped for a few hours in Resza [Riesa, Germany]. Resza at this time was populated by Jews, who had just learned that in the train yard was a whole train packed with other Jews, who were there, women, and children, and were sacrificing all their might to get some piece of bread to those on the path.

My brother yelled out, "Bring a little iodine!" because I was on the verge of death. And a little boy risked his life and threw in a little flask of iodine through the window, and I drank this, and the inflammation in my throat burst, and this is how my life was saved. But the little twelve-year-old boy who sacrificed his life and threw me the little iodine, unfortunately, the SS murderers shot him because they noticed him in the tumult, and they hunted him down and shot him.

After Resza, we kept on traveling and we came to a sudden halt in the middle of a field. We stayed in this field the whole night and through the next day. They said it was because of bombers in the vicinity and they would shoot at anyone. So they would send us to Russia. But what the real reason was we still don't know. But we knew one thing for sure, that we weren't far from the Russian border. And after staying still that night and day, the train started rolling again, but backward, until we were brought into Teschen [Czechoslovakia], where we were unloaded.

Three ambulances were set up in a row, the corpses were removed, and we were really relieved because it was announced that anyone not able to walk should declare this, and they'd be able to ride. I couldn't walk but my brother wouldn't let me declare this and he supported me like this until we were again forced onto a massive Czechoslovak military train. But they prevented us from getting aboard because the local passengers were waiting, so we were posted to the horse freight sections, the wooden barracks.

But this train was not really placed on the station rails, and to get to the linked cars was a very long walk. And at this time, Jews still lived in Czechoslovakia, and they found out about everything, so they wanted to bring us the bread anyone still had. But the guards wouldn't allow them near us. And if anyone dared throw any bread into our line, the SS would shoot them.

There was no straw in the wooden barracks, only the gravel we lay on. It was so crowded from so many people, one stepping over the next. And there we were given a little soup. And that was all. In Teschen, we stayed for four or six days, and afterward, we were again loaded onto the wagons and kept traveling. This time very briefly, and we were soon in Krakow. Krakow at the time still had Jews, and when we were led through the streets of Krakow, Jews managed to throw some bread through the windows, the little they had. But the Nazis wouldn't let us pick it up but beat us on our heads when we bent down to try to pick up the bread.

And this is how we were again led through Krakow into a camp. The camp was called Banaken. It was not really a camp but a large, open area of a factory with emptied buildings. There we were let out, and there the Jewish Community began feeding us, though not too much, at least to catch our breath, revived to live a little longer. We were guarded by SS commandos and we were there for a short time.

From there, after two weeks, the SS began taking out people to the Loszno Asylum, and there we were outfitted and given clothes and bathed, and led to another camp in Krakow, which was once the Polish Asylum for the Insane.

*[Henry's account of his first arrest and deportation abruptly ends here around November/December 1939. His later writing in English of the First Days of the War provides additional details—see above.]*

*[Henry continues his account of his second arrest and deportation to Auenrode slave labor camp in Germany November 11, 1940, to April 1941.]*

... Later, they marched us through the streets of Nuremberg, where people laughed at us as if we were animals. We spent a long time in Nuremberg.

From there they sent me to Auenrode [*Avenrue Krisgotka*]. There I worked on the R.A.B., that's where they built the Autostrade. I worked at paving and building strips, laying out the varieties. Work there was extremely hard, and [there was] not enough to eat. There was a slightly better camp there: every prisoner had his own bed and straw sack and a head board. And once a week, laundry was distributed, and you could wash yourself every day. In this camp,

Auenrode, I stayed from November 1940 until April 1941. I became ill from the blows I received from the work guards. And every Sunday, when we didn't work the main shift, we used aluminum to fasten long walls. Winter you had to run outside naked and roll out in the snow. And then they opened the yard to receive my pair of [shoes], beating, falling, trampling. My bladder was damaged. I couldn't hold any urine in it, couldn't feel when I vacated in my pants, and I had problems with my heart from all these tortures. On April 10, 1941, I was sent on a sick transport to Sosnowiec in a subcamp. This is what it was called.

*[Henry continues his account of his return home to Siewierz and then relocation to the Zawiercie Ghetto with his family, April 1941 to October 1943.]*

[April 1941] I returned home to Siewierz and then in [June 1942] I was sent to Zawiercie outside the Ghetto with my parents. And there in the Zawiercie Ghetto, I worked in the Luftwaffe Lager until October 1943, when I was sent to Auschwitz. My parents and brother were burned alive there by the murderous Nazis, may their memory be expunged. We were seven children at home, six brothers and only one sister, and three brothers were already married and every one of them had children.

*Aussiedlung* [Relocation]

Then an order came down from two SS officers, that we can soon expect a number of civilian Poles, and they will exchange their clothes with ours, and no resistance should be mounted; otherwise, we'll be shot. And immediately, civilian Poles came and they dragged away from us our good shoes, good linen, good shirts, and they returned torn shoes, torn pants, torn shirts. And this was how we were left without money, without anything, naked and barefoot, and at the end they had taken away everything from us.

This was on Wednesday late during the night. On Thursday the Gestapo encircled the entire Ghetto. And from the Ghetto to the Factory you only had to pass one street. A massive amount of gendarmerie arrived, and Gestapo and hounds. And all night you could hear shooting inside the Ghetto. I, my parents and brothers were inside the Ghetto. And in the part where we lived, I and my brothers built a kind of bunker in the attic to hide in. But the bunker was too small because many families lived in this building, so not all of us could hide. We only kept my parents there, and my sister and two younger brothers. I and my two married brothers didn't hide. I couldn't hide the two married brothers because of the children, because the children would have cried and they'd be found out. So the bunker would have been useless. I didn't sleep the whole night. As soon as day broke, we heard that everyone has to assemble on the large square by the Community Council. Everyone walked there, women, children, old and young.

The Germans killed the chairman of the Jewish Council and the commander of the Jewish Police with which the three Gestapo had just dined and drank a few hours ago, and this was how they killed them several hours later with boards, not wanting to waste a bullet. And like this, almost corpses they were thrown straight into the wagons with all the other people. And I was still standing on the square and witnessed it all. Everyone had already been led away.

This lieutenant of the Luftwaffe comes over to us, and he took command of us, and led us into the Luftwaffe, not the wagons. And he told us we would remain here in the Luftwaffe for work and we would sleep here. There remained from the whole Ghetto after the general *Aussiedlung* about seven hundred people, all young people without children. Not one solitary child was left alive. When we entered the Luftwaffe, the murderers had already sent all the people away. The only hope that I had was that I'd be able to help out my parents and two brothers and my younger sister a little, who all lay hidden in the bunker. And this was why I struggled so hard to survive. But all my work was in vain. The Ghetto continued to be under strict control and guard by the SS, and they kept up their hunt for people. The SS and their hounds.

And they managed to find many more people. On Friday, the SS found many people in the bunker and they were dragged away to the square, to the Jewish Council. And the lieutenant of the Luftwaffe was not the worst, so he went over there and saved the younger people with the approval of the Gestapo, and he brought them into the Luftwaffe for labor. I went over to the lieutenant and told him about my parents, brothers, and sister, and that he should help me. So he assured he would help me. He said he had to wait a little until the whole *Aussiedlung* finished and cooled down, and he would get them out. I was extremely relieved because I knew that they had enough food for a few days, and when it gets quieter the Gestapo would leave the Ghetto and it would be easier to get them out of the bunker and bring them into the camp. But in the meantime, things changed.

Shabbos someone informed at the Gestapo about the bunker, and they went there and dragged all the people away to the square. And there were already a few hundred people there. So I ran to the Luftwaffe lieutenant for him to rescue my parents, brothers, and sister out of the Gestapo's grip, but, unfortunately, he had taken a weekend leave and there was no one who could help from the Luftwaffe.

So we could see through the windows all that was happening on the square, and I witnessed my parents, brothers, and sister how they were stranded on the square, and the dogs were mauling them so, and I'm standing like this and cannot help them. I simply went mad from all this. I ran back and forth and begged the murderers to rescue them. I can still see them before my eyes today. I will never forget this image as long as I live. Others tried to console me that before they would be taken to Auschwitz, they would be brought to the Luftwaffe and maybe they would be able to be rescued from there. Before it became dark, they started leading all of them to the Luftwaffe, and the coal wagons were already assembled for the people.

And there Shabbos night, the first of Selichos 1943, they were led and deported to Auschwitz for extermination. I wanted to break away to the place they were being loaded, or drag them away, or travel with them, but the Luftwaffe soldiers prevented my reaching them. And this was the last time I saw my parents, two brothers, and only sister. I never saw them again. I cried and screamed all night. I wanted to jump through the window, but I was guarded.

This is what the *Aussiedlung* looked like.

The Gestapo with the hounds drove us to cxhaustion, the dogs tore us apart. I can still hear the screams and the crying of the small children ringing in my ears. Then they lined the people up into rows. And this is how they kept up this pulling people out of the Ghetto, to the Luftwaffe, to the Factory. The freight trains were already set up in the Luftwaffe, and this was how they pushed the people inside the wagons and sealed the cars shut. And later, the count was short because they, the Gestapo, took a meal break, for the Gestapo, not, forbid the thought, for the poor little children, who were whimpering and screaming for a drop of milk or a little water. The Gestapo stomped on these Jewish children with their heavy boots and the screams were so loud they reached the heavens. Who can understand this and who can believe this, that people can do this. They took living, breathing Jewish children and they were stuffed into sacks and tied up and thrown like this into the coal wagons. And the poor mothers and fathers stood by like this and witnessed all this and were powerless. But the Gestapo took the smallest children and tore them in half, then threw them back at the mothers. Or took Jewish children, held them by the feet, and they smashed their heads into walls until the small Jewish head was shattered. Can anyone imagine this? After a few hours' interruption, they again commanded everyone to assemble into rows.

I and my brothers were trying to push as hard as we could to be the last ones; maybe some miracle will happen. But no miracle happened. I saw that we were approaching the last people and the end of the line was reaching me. Then I saw that on the other side they were calling out craftsmen, and they got kept separately. I then heard them call out some name a few times and no one stepped forward. So I ran off and declared myself and I stood myself in the line of the separately called.

And I stood like this until the last transport of people was led out to the Luftwaffe, to the wagons—it was approaching the end.

My two married brothers with their wives and children were sent out seven weeks before me from the Ghetto, they, during the *Aussiedlung.* My eldest brother had four children. The second eldest had two children, and the third eldest had one child. I was the youngest of the brothers. My sister was younger than I by three years. This was how the Nazi murderers annihilated, incinerated, and tortured them in Auschwitz.

This was related to me by eyewitness accounts before I was deported to Auschwitz: My brothers Srulik and Herschel, along with a group of other young men, were taken by the SS to load up all the dead bodies of Jews lying on the streets in town and bring them to the Jewish cemetery. There they were ordered to dig a mass grave and throw the bodies in it. When the group finished, the SS shot each and every one of the men, including my two brothers, Srulik and Herschel.

*[Henry was on the last transport of Jews from the Zawiercie Ghetto on October 18, 1943. Henry was registered in Auschwitz as #157756 under the name Szlama Rosenblatt, born August 2, 1920. He made these changes to his name and year of birth to hide his identity because the SS in Siewierz were looking for him because of his black-market activities. On November 14, 1943, Henry was transferred to the Auschwitz subcamp Lagischa.]*

Auschwitz—So for me, a new chapter started. We were undressed from head to foot and shorn and washed and given the number on the arm. My number was 157756. They took our clothes away. We were handed the striped uniforms with the wooden clogs for shoes, and we slept on wooden slats. Seven people to one perch, three levels high. One on top of the other. We were fed once a day a little salt water. We practically looked like skeletons. We worked very hard all day long. At night we were tortured; our feet were burned by fire. Hung by our arms and beaten. Not a bit of it can be repeated. And from there, Auschwitz, we were sent to Lagischa for labor to build the Elektrizitatswerke. This was not far from Auschwitz. It belonged to Auschwitz I, one subcamp of Auschwitz. Here it was very bad. From this camp very few people survived. Every few weeks new victims were brought in for labor and they dropped like flies. Jews were brought from Holland, from France, Italy; all died. Tortured. Shot. They couldn't survive these few weeks, the misery. I was already used to the suffering. Every day the black limousine carried away half-dead people to Auschwitz to burn. This was life in Lagischa. I was there until they liquidated the camp because the Russians started making advances. So the SS liquidated the camp. We were sent to Golleschau and there I worked in coal pits very miserably.

*[From Golleschau Henry was sent back to Auschwitz and then forced on to the Death March to Blechhammer, Buchenwald and ultimately Flossenbürg concentration camp where he was liberated in April 1945.]*

## HENRY ROSENBLATT—LAGISCHA LABOR CAMP—SUBCAMP OF AUSCHWITZ

*[Report recorded by Helena Chain of the Jewish Historical Commission in Będzin taken shortly after his arrival in Będzin in May 1945.]*

Henryk Rosenblatt describes the persecution that he had to endure, according to his rendition in the Lagischa camp. [36]

Log of the report from Henryk Rosenblatt [37] recorded by Helena Chaim[38] Jewish Historical Commission in Będzin. [39]

---

[36] The document was translated from Polish.

[37] Henryk Rosenblatt, later Henry Rosenblatt (1919), trunk maker, was arrested in 1939 in Siewierz and carried off to forced labor. In October 1943 he was deported from the Zawiercie Ghetto to Auschwitz. From there he was transferred to the Lagischa camp and Jaworzno; and to Flossenbürg in January 1945, where he was freed in April 1945. He emigrated to the United States in 1951 and was a businessman in New York.

[38] Helena Chaim (1907), teacher from Będzin.

[39] Henryk Rosenblatt reported this from his experience to the Jewish Commission

The Lagischa Camp:

During the war, I lived in Zawiercie. On September 25, 1943 [actual date was October 18, 1943], I was deported to Auschwitz-Birkenau. I stayed there for two weeks. Because they needed a shipment of younger, healthier people for the building of an electricity plant in Lagischa, they chose one hundred of us for this purpose. [40] We drove there in two trucks. The trip lasted only an hour, because Lagischa is only thirty-five kilometers distant from Auschwitz. On October 9, 1943 [actual date was November 14, 1943], we arrived in Lagischa. There were already Jewish people there for the building of the electricity plant, others for the building of railroad tracks, in total about eight hundred. With the same trucks, the Germans brought about 150 sick and weak Jewish people, as well as the dead, back to Auschwitz. The sick had been in Lagischa for about two weeks. They fared so poorly here that they were soon at their end. We arrived Sunday afternoon in Lagischa and stood in the yard until night. It poured rain. At night they brought us into a not-yet-finished block. There were neither windows nor a floor. The camp had over three barracks in total. We stayed along the wall and waited for commands. A Jewish overseer (kapo) came and told us we should be sorry to have landed here, because here you would be done. The work would be hard, we would be beaten, we would receive nothing to eat, and the guards would be ruthless. A half hour later came the German block leader (Blockführer) named Schmid. [41] He was small, and there was an ironic smile on his face. He asked us who came from Lodz and sold "hot Bajgelech and hot sausage." [42] We answered that none of us were from Lodz. Additionally

---

probably shortly after his arrival in Będzin in May 1945.

[40] In the Lagischa camp (today in the district of Będzin), there were more than one hundred Jewish prisoners from Auschwitz used for the building of the power station "Walter" for the energy supply of Upper Silesia.

[41] Josef Schmid (1922), mason; German from Bácsalmás, Hungary. In 1942 he was drafted into the SS. He was employed in the Jawischowitz and Kobier camps from September 1943 to July 1944. He was block leader in Lagischa, thereafter block leader in Monowitz and Gleiwitz. In 1947 he was sentenced to seven years of detention in the district court of Wadowice. He was released in 1953 and worked as a mason and doorman in Hofheim; in 1981 he was sentenced to eight years of detention in Frankfurt am Main.

[42] In original German.

he commanded to the kapo next to him that he should search us, even though we stood before him in prisoners' clothing. During the search each of us received a blow to the stomach and to the chest. Ten from our hundred were brought to the infirmary. Then the kapo commanded us to lie on our stomachs, and so we did, until Schmid came back. The kapo stood there and guarded us; he did not allow us to stand up because he was afraid of this swine [i.e., Schmid]. After about an hour, Schmid came and told us to stand up. He approached everyone, looked him in the eye, laughed demonically, and asked everyone about his occupation. No answer pleased him. If one told him he was a tailor, Schmid beat him. This procedure lasted two hours. When he left, we were left tired and battered to sleep on the floor. In the morning at 4:00 we were awakened. The kapo woke us as a bell-toll. He let us know that everyone but our group would now get bread, because there were not enough rations for us. We drank cold, unsweetened coffee. At 5:00 came the command: "Work detail begin." Thereupon one had to run quickly to the square in front of the gate. Because we didn't yet know the meaning of this command, we went slowly and didn't know why they beat us again. Thereafter they commanded us to line up, and each kapo chose people for the work detail.

He chose me to work outside the camp, to unload the building materials from train cars. The tracks were in the woods. Our convoy included fifty people and one kapo. With us came also four SS guards, who supervised us. As we went through the gate, we again received beatings because we did not hold up our arms. To the column that I was divided into belonged two experienced Jewish prisoners. They looked around secretly in order to determine which SS guards accompanied us. Later during the work, they informed us that there were four SS guards in the camp who had the mission of killing four people. From those who were going with us belonged only one of these four [guards]. That comforted us a little. We hoped that this one would be influenced by the other three. And that's the way it was. We walked to a shed in which we found shovels and pickaxes. The kapo divided us to work. Four each were organized to a wagon, in order to unload iron, wood, stone, and cement. When those who had less material were finished, the SS guards beat the others, so that they would be done quicker. The work lasted from 6:00 a.m. to 6:00 p.m. The path to the work lasted an hour, and because of that, we left at 5:00 a.m. in order to be punctual. At 6:00 was the muster. We were counted off, then they practiced with us, "Hat off, hat on." [43] Then we went into a trot to the barracks. It consisted of one big hall, in which there were eight hundred men. We received dinner, soup from cabbage leaves and nettles. We were very hungry. They announced second helpings. Everyone crowded themselves to the soup pails. The block elder (Blockälteste) beat everyone who came for more soup. Meanwhile the block leader entered and ordered the rest of the soup to be thrown away in the garbage. That was done. At 8:00 p.m., they divided up for us 250 grams of bread and a little jam. At 9:00 p.m. was muster; the Blockälteste counted us off and ordered us to fall asleep. The light was turned off. At 10:00 p.m. he came back and checked the cleanliness of our legs. Whether one had clean or dirty legs, everyone had to get up, lie over a stool, and receive twenty-five canings. This theater lasted until after 1:00. We wept from pain. This horrible affair was kept up over four weeks, until a new transport with Jewish men from France arrived. These were three hundred people who were going to take care of themselves. After three weeks, from these three hundred people, only sixty remained. At night the block leader checked our tin bowls and threw a wrench at our heads.

After two weeks came a new Blockälteste. In the winter, at first, the barrack room was heated at night. When the master claimed we had been working poorly, the workers had to crawl the whole path on our stomachs through the snow. When we came back to the camp, we had to work for another three hours. At first there was no infirmary. There was also no doctor. A nurse had to work during the day [on site]; at night he applied bandages. After approximately two months, an office was set up that could take fifteen sick people. Then there arrived a Jewish doctor. Very many sick people died. Two months later came Obersturmführer Schwarz [44] from Auschwitz and he went through a selection. He chose two hundred people

[43] From the original German ("*Mütze ab, Mütze auf*").

[44] As camp commander from Auschwitz III in November 1943, Heinrich Schwarz was also responsible for the subcamps at armament companies.

for Auschwitz, who were picked up two days later by a truck. With the same truck were brought new workers from Auschwitz. They reported to the doctor at night between 7:00 and 8:00 p.m. The master maintained the work tempo. Additionally they divided us up for the building of a reservoir in the camp. When it was done, the block leader frequently threw workers into it. When the Blockälteste found a dirty plate left by somebody, that person had to undress, go out into the snow, and lie for an hour under the cold water faucet. When we went through the city, it sometimes happened that someone would throw us a piece of bread. If someone picked it up, he was instantly shot. The camp was surrounded by a triple barbed-wire fence, which was loaded with electricity and on which were fit lamps in close succession. In between there were guardhouses, in which SS guards always sat. The victims died from hunger and sickness. The food was never better, even at the end. In the pre-harvesttime we went three days without any bread. We had to get by with soup. On the fourth day the master asked us the reason for our weakness during our work. We told him everything. He thereupon yelled at the squad leader (Kommandoführer). In the afternoon at 2:00 came a vehicle with bread to the electricity plant. In May 1944 there arrived a transport with Jewish Hungarians from Auschwitz. Two hundred thirteen- and fourteen-year-old boys had to perform the same work as us. There were therefore many deaths. By August there were 180 left from the newcomers. In August 1944, as the Russians neared Warsaw, the Germans transported machines and material to Berlin. In September they sent us to the camp Neu-Dachs. [45]

[45] In Neu-Dachs (Jaworzno) the energy supply of Upper Silesia built another power plant and operated it since June 1943 as a subcamp from Auschwitz, which counted over three thousand prisoners in August 1944.

6. März ... 3.

U. m. Akten
dem Herrn Oberstaatsanwalt
als Leiter der Anklagebehörde
bei dem Sondergericht
in O p p e l n

mit folgender Ausserung zurückgereicht.
Die 250 in Siewierz wohnhaft gewesenen Juden wurden durch das einzige jüdische Lebensmittelgeschäft des Mendel Israel Rosenblat mit Lebensmitteln versorgt. Die Zuweisung, sowie die Abrechnung derselben erfolgte direkt durch die jüdische Kultusgemeinde in Warthenau, sodaß das hiesige Wirtschafts- und Ernährungsamt mit dem Geschäft Rosenblat grundsätzlich nichts zu tun hatte.
In der Nacht vom 16. zum 17.6.42 fand die Aussetzung der hiesigen Juden, ohne meine vorherige Benachrichtigung statt. Erst am Vormittag der Aussetzung wurde mir amtlich mitgeteilt, dass die Juden Siewierz räumen müssen und wie ich mich hinsichtlich des zurückgelassenen Vermögens zu verhalten habe.

March 6, 1943 letter with Nazi Stamp for the Zaglembie Region requesting compensation for the food Mendel Rosenblatt, Henry's father, took for the 250 Jews who were resettled from Siewierz on June 16 and 17, 1942

Konzentrationslager AUSCHWITZ — Art der Haft: Pol. Jude — Gef. Nr. 157756

Name und Vorname: Rosenblatt Szlama Israel
geb.: 1.8.1920 zu: Siewierz
Wohnort: Warthenau
Beruf: Maler — Rel.: mos.
Staatsangehörigkeit: ehem. Polen — Stand: led.
Name der Eltern: — Rasse: jüd.
Wohnort:
Name der Ehefrau: — Rasse:
Wohnort:
Kinder: — Alleiniger Ernährer der Familie oder der Eltern:
Vorbildung:
Militärdienstzeit: — von – bis
Kriegsdienstzeit: — von – bis
Grösse: 170 — Nase: gewellt — Haare: schwarz — Gestalt: schlank
Mund: klein — Bart: — Gesicht: oval — Ohren: normal
Sprache: poln. deutsch — Augen: braun — Zähne:
Ansteckende Krankheit oder Gebrechen: keine
Besondere Kennzeichen: keine
Rentenempfänger:

Verhaftet am: — wo:
1. Mal eingeliefert: 18. 4. 43 — 2. Mal eingeliefert:
Einweisende Dienststelle:

Henry Rosenblatt's Auschwitz Registration Card

## ENDNOTE

# MY MOTHER: A FIGHTER WHO NEVER FAILED TO AMAZE

This project was initiated by my sister Lillian with the full support of my brother Melvin and myself. It had been my mother's longstanding desire to write her memoirs and we wanted to fulfill her wish. As the project unfolded over this past year, I became more and more involved and ultimately decided to write it with her. The hours we spent going over her story, clarifying and verifying details, sorting through her pictures, and identifying people helped both of us get through an extremely difficult time of our lives with the untimely death of my youngest brother Melvin and the isolation caused by the coronavirus pandemic.

My mother is a fighter who has never failed to amaze everyone with her strength and love of life. She truly believes that there is always some good out there, and writing her memoir with her once again showed her amazing ability to adapt and make the best out of terrible situations. It was an answer to our most trying days.

We all heard her story in bits and pieces over the years, but the challenge was to write it down in a linear timeline and framework to better understand her experience during the Holocaust. I who knew her stories better than anyone learned something new every day. And every week, I found historical documents and confirmation of her smallest details. It was an incredible journey for me.

I thank my mother for her incredible memory and recall, her desire to share every detail and her patience with my constant questions and prodding. I am honored to be her daughter and appreciate the gifts that she has given me, now and always. As much as this memoir might appear to be our gift to her, this was truly her biggest gift to me.

My mother's true strength is her ability to bear every adversity and accept the unimaginable, combined with her unconditional love for her family.

Belinda Rosenblatt Levavi

September 2020

## POSTSCRIPTS

I could write volumes on my mother, but I will keep it succinct. My associations with my mother, Mira, have many chapters since she has been my mother for sixty-nine years. As a young girl I remember her energy, her spirit, her hard work and her playfulness. She rose early and went to bed late. She took care of many of the household responsibilities and expected us to do likewise. She was a perfectionist and expected similar from her children. My mother preached "start your day making your bed" as a good life practice way before it was in fashion. Despite this serious-mindedness she would at times surprise us and be playful and adventurous; building snow forts, making snow angels, and sledding were her initiatives. Spending hours playing in our backyard and giving us the freedom to explore the neighborhoods of Springfield with her permission. Summers were often spent roving around with a number of other kids for most of the day and showing up around dinnertime. She trusted us to be "good kids."

My parents worked hard and expected us to contribute. As young children and teens we didn't always appreciate that expectation. They encouraged us to be independent and discover the world. My mother has always been curious of people and places. She genuinely enjoys learning about others and their experiences. Despite her tragic early life story, she believes in the potential goodness of people. She is loyal and fights on behalf of her friends. My parents were forced to grow up way before their time and in some ways expected likewise of me, which led to me being an avid traveler and having a strong interest in other people and cultures.

My mother was beautiful, elegant, and always had many admirers. She liked to look and dress well and receive compliments, but always did it in a very understated manner. She preferred to rely on her intelligence and be known for her solid judgement. She loved flowers and beauty; her house has always been filled with beautiful plants, and when we lived in Springfield, she always grew flowers. Every time I see a beautiful flower, I recall her pleasure

in their color and scent. She loved to cook and bake, and had quite a reputation for making delicious cakes. She was generous in her hospitality and always welcomed friends and others to our home, a quality that I have continued in my own home.

For my parents, their children have been their wealth. Over our many years we have been told repeatedly how much we meant to them, and that nothing can happen to us since they have lost so much already. I accepted it as my life's responsibility to stay alive and help others. I never felt burdened by it, it just seemed to be a fact of life. Somehow it was up to us, to soften some of the blows that life had dealt my parents.

My mother's warmth and her openness in expressing her love for us has always made us feel secure. She ends most phone calls with "I love you." She was always the one who remembered everyone's birthday and anniversary, and would make sure that my father sent us these flowery cards in his difficult to decipher script.

This year, my mother does not remember the date of my birthday which has saddened her. However, she said to me "I may not remember the date like I always used to but I remember it in my Heart."

That's my mother, the fighter with a big heart!

Lillian Rosenblatt Fischler
September 2020

# IN MEMORIAM

## Melvin's Last Note [partial]

I remember the fun times, playing in the snow and making snow angels. I always knew how hard Dad and you worked to sustain the family. Those times you took off from work were hard to come by and you always made them available. As the years went by, everyone got older and went their separate ways. During that time, I watched you struggle to keep the family together and how hard you worked to accomplish that. I often recount how much money and effort you and Dad put into this effort–gathering the family for Pesach in Florida to bring us together–to make sure we were a cohesive family.

Mom, I have long enduring memories of our wonderful times together. Think of me as someone who has always loved you dearly and has always invested whatever time I could in helping you. My time has come to a finish, your time will continue. Enjoy the things that will come yet, such as additional great-grandchildren. I love you.

**Sara:** Melvin loved his mother so much that it was absolutely amazing to see a child have that much love for a parent. And I love Mira because she gave me the greatest gift of all, my best friend and life partner, Melvin.

Melvin Rosenblatt
September 29, 2019

## MY LEGACY

# GRANDCHILDREN

### **Ruvin Levavi**, born August 6, 1983

Our Bubbe is the living embodiment and definition of the power of love. She had her childhood and family ripped away from her, yet her emotions and spirit are always hers. She rebuilt generations starting with her love for her husband, children, grandchildren and my kids–her great-grandchildren. I always thought I was her favorite, that her love for me was the strongest. As her first grandchild, I felt she loved me more than everyone else. Hence, she loves my wife the most, and my kids the most. How wrong I was.

Her love for my Zaide after the desolation of the Holocaust was on another level. In his later years I had the opportunity to take a "boys" trip with my Zaide to Israel. Well into their eighties, Bubbe called every night; she gave me a moment but focused her attention on him, repeatedly doting on him and telling her how much she missed and loved him.

It all started there. Bubbe's ability to find love with Zaide gave her the opportunity to pass that on to the rest of us. The strength of that love makes

us all feel the most important, the most loved. Her zest for life and need for family connection is felt in every interaction. It is evidenced every time we visit her through every goodbye. I am thirty-seven and it's been the same for as long as I can remember. We say goodbye at the door of her fifth-floor apartment. Bubbe refuses to close the door; we await the elevator as she continues to shout down the hallway how much she loves us. The elevator arrives, we again yell goodbye. As we board the elevator and it begins to descend, we can still hear her professing her love for us. That love and its perseverance will follow us always.

## **Zev Levavi,** born November 29, 1986

Bubbe has lived so many lives. She has been a daughter, a sister, a wife, a mother, a grandmother, and a great-grandmother. She is a survivor. She has seen almost ten full decades. It is hard to fathom how much history, personal and global, she has lived through during that time. It is impossible to put into words her role in my past, present, and future. My memory is full of the sights, sounds, and smells of her home and her cooking. She taught me how to love through food. Her vegetable soup warmed me during winters and her blueberry pies felt like summer. Bubbe also showed me the meaning of grace. She is a stylish woman and she has a beautiful way with people. She has a wry smile and a playful twinkle in her eye, windows into her childhood stories of Sosnowiec.

Bubbe has been telling her story for a long time. It connects her to the past and gives meaning to the future. When I was young, her story scared me. I was overwhelmed by the trauma and I had night terrors of uniformed Nazis and deportations. As I grew older, I realized that there were gifts in her tellings. Her unbreakable moral compass and humanist compassion are the ones I try to take with me every day. Bubbe is the strongest person I know. I love her and I have always felt her love with me.

## Abe Levavi, born July 8, 1988

I've always had a strong bond with my grandmother, my Bubbe. When I think of her, my mind is flooded with memories from my childhood. Memories of going to her and my Zaide's house in Sackett Lake on Friday afternoons for pre-shabbos vegetable soup, always with "fresh" bread. Of the times we would play kickball in the front yard of that same house, as we waited for the day camp bus. Or the times she would explain to people that I was her "fox" and that I would have "survived," as I shifted uncomfortably nearby. Of her apple pie, and how she would watch closely as you took the first bites to see if it was up to standard.

But more than my childhood memories, what I love most about my Bubbe is how she has stayed flexible in her outlook after all these years. It sounds small, but in the most important moments, she has been there to support me and my decisions, even when those decisions have not squared with her worldview. The ability for a person to grow and be flexible after all that she has been through is remarkable, and what I most admire.

## Gabe Fischler, born May 4, 1995

I'd like to share two experiences of mine with Bubbe and Zaide that are significant to me:

1. During my trip to Poland in January 2013, I would have long nightly phone conversations with them. I remember hearing stories of Zaide's brothers and hometown before visiting the site of his brothers' graves and his childhood home. Having their stories fresh in my mind while visiting places that were of such significance to them is something I will never forget.
2. The Saxony Hotel and chocolate lollipops. Getting the family together for Pesach was so important to my grandparents. I remember them as always being at the head of the table for every meal and playing shuffleboard with us. Most importantly, though, were the chocolate lollipop trips. Every two or

so hours, my brother, my cousin Matthew, and I would run upstairs to their room and hang out on their balcony eating chocolate lollipops with them.

Everything they've taught me over the years as well as their endless love and support has truly helped me to be the person I am today.

## Danny Fischler, born July 29, 1998

I have many significant memories with my grandmother, and there are definitely many that will stick with me forever. Running to her room for chocolate lollipops and other Kosher for Passover candy, and her making her amazing soup whenever we visited. There are also memories of her stories of the Holocaust and her incredible life. Her stories of survival and courage will stick with me forever. I remember listening to her stories while playing with toys in their apartment for hours, listening to how her and Zaide met, and the horrible cruelties that she was forced to endure. I do not know what I will remember most about Bubbe later in life, but I will always remember her love and her hugs and affection, and everything she and Zaide did for me.

## Danielle Rosenblatt Mendelsohn, born January 5, 1989

My grandmother, Mira Rosenblatt, has redefined "strength" for me over and over again throughout our years together. She has overcome horrors that I hope to never hear of in our lifetime, and survived against all odds with a will that I wish I could find even a spark of. She never ceases to amaze me, but when looking at this woman, you would never know.

She has always been dressed to the T. All the beautifully coordinated jewelry and signature hair style, jet black set perfectly on the top of her head. As a little girl I loved watching her clip in her hair net with these funny looking clips before bed and emptying a bottle of hairspray into it. I loved sleeping over at my Bubbe and Zaide's house and bringing toys into their bed to play between them in the early morning. I loved staying over for shabbat and listening to my grandfather demand that he be allowed to help in the kitchen as this was his kitchen too!

Not only was this an opportunity to spend quality time with my grandparents, but also a chance for me to get to know my father as a child. I would stay in his room with his coded lock he had engineered as a child in efforts to lock out his sisters. His first test tubes and medical materials, knickknacks, treasures and keepsakes were all around me and gave me insight into the childhood of a very dedicated doctor and father that is recently no longer with us.

We spent every Pesach together in Florida with my grandparents and father's side of the family. It was there, at the hotels, at these seders, where I learned most about my grandparents and the characteristics and values they wished to imbue upon me. As the only granddaughter, I was held to a high level of expectation and accomplishment. To my grandmother, intelligence was synonymous with education and survival, and without it, well, that wasn't an option. As hard as I may have fought this as a child, I could not be more grateful for this direction as an adult.

My Heritage trip to Poland brought their stories that I was raised on to life; making their insistence on education, respect, and properness abundantly clear, and indeed of the utmost importance. I was able to walk through those gates of Auschwitz and out. Something that much of my family was never allowed to do and still remain there in the ashes. The black wrought iron words "Arbeit macht frei" are not cruel and savage irony, but rather an empowering mantra that ensured survival for many, especially my family, and still does to this day. It is their experiences there and during that time, which transformed them into the people that they are, and they continue to transform those around them, leaving the lasting message of "Never Again."

## **Jonathan Rosenblatt,** born February 26, 1993

Bubbe taught me the value of "self" and the importance of looking out for yourself. It is hard for me to think of Bubbe without thinking about the Holocaust. I can't remember ever speaking with her when we didn't talk about what she went through during those years. We might start a conversation about other things, but it always veered into a story about her past. At times, it was difficult for me to listen as much as I wanted to be respectful. I know that I am lucky that I never had to live through what Bubbe went through.

## **Matthew Rosenblatt,** born December 2, 1998

I was the youngest grandchild, so I saw my Bubbe differently than my cousins. She didn't play ball with me, but she was always ready to listen to me read or play number games. Bubbe believed in education and being proper, and taught me how to work hard and be motivated. She wanted all of us to strive for success, and she was our inspiration. Bubbe was beautiful and she prided herself on dressing well and looking good. I think I get my fashion sense from her.

My ninety-seven-year-old Bubbe stood for hours in her hot kitchen teaching me how to bake her sugar cookies after I mentioned how much I loved them. She was always willing to do and give me things to show her love. And she gave me my father [Melvin], which was the most special of all gifts. He loved her so much and I have learned how to be a loving person from both of them.

ADDENDA

# HISTORICAL FAMILY BACKGROUND

## Family of Łęczycki/ Lenczycki

Łęczyca is a city about thirty-five miles north-west of Łodz. Jews came to this area of Poland from Spain in times of the King Casimir the Great (1333-1370). At the end of the 18th century, Jews had to choose their family name. Before this time, they were called: Joseph son of .... They paid for the name and it was often chosen from the place they lived or from nature; for example, Rosenblatt (rose leaf). That is how the name Lenczycki came to be the family name.

The family moved to Łask which was twenty miles south-west of Łódz around the mid-1800s because of disease and fires in Łęczyca.

## Marriage Certificate Dated 1861 Translated from Old Polish

Haim and Ludka Rajzla Łęczycki were merchants and lived in Łask. Their son Manel Łęczycki, single and twenty-one years old, married Hendla Sieradzka, single and twenty years old, from the city Sieradz. Hendla's parents were Abram Leib and her deceased mother Gitla Sieradzki. They lived in Burzonin, a city near Łódz.

The wedding took place in Burzonin on December 18, 1861 at 5 o'clock in the afternoon. The religious Jewish ceremony was officiated by deputy Rabbi Aron Pinkus Kempinski. Before the ceremony there were three banns in the Synagogues of Łask and Burzonin. No one was against the marriage. The certificate was read and signed by two witnesses: Haim Grinbaum and Shlomo Mandelman. Rabbi Aron Pinkus Kempinski and the town clerk also signed.

## Łask to Lututow to Łodz

The family of Haim and Ludka Lenczycki moved from Łask to Lututow and finally to Łodz. Their son Manel Łęczycki and his wife Hendla had three sons: Mordechai Wolf, Henoch and Moshe who was born in Lututow.

- Mordechai Wolf Łęczycki married Baila Yehudis Abromowicz from Sielec, a city outside of Sosnowiec. They lived in Łask and their first child, my mother Hendla, was born there. They moved to Sosnowiec where their other eight children were born.
- Henoch Łęczycki married Miriam Lewkowicz. Their children were Shimon/Simon and Abram (both survived and lived in Australia); and Helcha (who married my uncle Shaya). Henoch died in the Łodz Ghetto in 1944.
- Moshe Łęczycki married Mira Unikowski. They had six children: Bluma, Israel, Róża and Hela born in Łask; David (Moshe Lavy's father who survived and lived in Israel) and Gita, born in Lututów.

The Łęczycki, Unikowski and Lewkowicz families were very close and the cousins played together throughout their childhood. Later some marriages were arranged between the cousins.

## Family of Rozenblat/Rosenblatt

**Leibisch Rosenblatt** married **Leah Ginsburg** and they lived in Siewierz. They had five children: Mendel (Henry's father); Chil; Chaya, Chava; and Surela.

- Mendel, Henry's father born March 13, 1886 married his cousin Chaja Rozenblat born November 11, 1880. They had six children: Jacob/Yankel born January 22, 1906; Abram; Wolf; Israel/Srulik born November 4, 1913; Herszlik born November 18, 1916; Chil born August 2, 1919; and Sura born July 10, 1923. Henry's mother Chaja died around 1930 and his father Mendel married Marjem Bankier from Wolbrom.
- Chil married Rivka Panski from Będzin. They survived and lived

in New York. They had six children: Mary Schreiber; Millie Vorhand; Betty Retter; Margot Pollack; Leah Eisenberg; and a son who died in England.

- Chaya married her cousin Berisch Rozenblat who died young. She then married Pinkus Helberg. There were four children: Moshe; Yankel; Berisch; Rivkele. No one survived.
- Chava married Pincus Wajcman and lived in Siewierz. They had four boys: Israel; Herschel born December 15, 1916; Mayer; and Motchek. Only Herschel Wajcman survived and lived in Israel.
- Surela married David Schlesinger from Dombrowa. They had four children: Yentil; Esther; Chana; and Shlomo. Shlomo survived and lived in New York.

The Sosnowiec Court Archive has a document on file signed by Abram Lenczycki dated May 31, 1946. Abram attested that his sister Hendla/Helena Rozenblat (my mother) born in Łask on February 13, 1895 to the parents of Wolf and Baja Ides was shot to death while trying to escape from the gathering place in the beginning of August 1942. However, Hendla was NOT shot to death; she was deported with her husband, my father, Shlomo Yitzhak, to Auschwitz from the Dulag in Sosnowiec on August 13-14, 1942. The apartment building on Targowa 21 was under Hendla's name and Abram needed to provide proof of her death to obtain ownership of the property.

There is a strong possibility that my sister Esther and my brother Natan used a combination of my parents' and grandparents' names to register for housing in the Srodula ghetto because they were so young. Szaja Szlama Rozenblat b. February 28, 1880 is registered as #152 and Breindla Rozenblat b. May 20, 1883 is registered as #153 on an official relocation list of Jews to the Srodula ghetto between February 17 and 22, 1943.

("Verzeichnie No. 10 der Juden, welche aus dem Bereucg des II. Pol. Rev. nach dem III. Pol. Rev./ Schrodel/in der zeir vom: 17-22.2.43. Doersiedelt wurde," Number 25.)

It was unbelievable at my age to learn new information about my family but the database of Jewish Records Indexing–Poland provided new details. I discovered that my grandparents Mordechaj Wolf Lenczycki (Wolek Łęczycki) and Bajla Ides Yehudit Abramowicz had ten children not nine like I always thought. They had a daughter who died young; that my uncle Moniek and my uncle Shaya were twins; and that I had confused the birth order of my aunts and uncles.

The birth records showed the following: my mother Helena (Hendla), born February 13, 1895; Shimon Baer (Szymon Ber), unknown; Sura Fajga, born October 9, 1901 and died at five years and six months old; Shaya (Szaja) and Moniek (Moszek) were twins, born July 7, 1902; Rushka (Rajzla), born 1906; Franya (Frymeta), born 1907; Chamech (Chaim), born 1909; Henia, unknown; and Abram, born June 10, 1911. Additionally, my grandfather's occupation was listed as "tinsman" which matched his business of making copper gutters.

Made in the USA
Coppell, TX
09 March 2021